DAVID YERKES is a member of the Department of English and Comparative Literature at Columbia University.

At King Alfred's command, Bishop Wærferth of Worcester translated Gregory's *Dialogues* into English during the last quarter of the ninth century. About a century or a century and a half later, between 950 and 1050, someone, probably again at Worcester, went through the translation with painstaking care, making thousands of changes in vocabulary and phrasing. The anonymous reviser had constant recourse to a copy of Gregory's Latin, and some of his changes do in fact render the Latin more closely. The vast majority of the changes, though, were introduced apparently only to bring the translation's diction up to date or into conformity with that of the reviser's own dialect, since they do not make the translation more accurate. On occasion, however, neither of these explanations seems to apply. For instance, to translate *famulus* the reviser twice substituted *þeow* for *wer,* once *wer* for *þeow.* This may mean that, in the reviser's opinion, *þeow* and *wer* represented true synonyms – an Old English counterpart to Fowler's 'gorse' and 'furze'; more likely, the reviser felt some crucial difference in the context. But whatever the reason for the thousands of new words, when put alongside the old words of Wærferth's original translation, they form a sizable and unique Old English thesaurus.

the two versions of waerferth's translation of gregory's dialogues: an old english thesaurus

DAVID YERKES

published in association with
The Centre for Medieval Studies, University of Toronto,
by University of Toronto Press
Toronto Buffalo London

Toronto Buffalo London
Printed in Canada

Library of Congress Cataloging in Publication Data

Yerkes, David, 1950-
The two versions of Wærferth's translation
of Gregory's Dialogues.

(Toronto Old English series ; v. 4)
Bibliography: p. ix
Includes index.
1. Gregorius I, the Great, Saint, Pope, ca. 540-
604. Dialogi de Vita. 2. Wærferth, Bp. of Wor-
cester, d. 915. 3. Anglo-Saxon language – Glossaries,
vocabularies, etc. 4. Latin language, Postclassical
– Glossaries, vocabularies, etc. I. Title.
II. Series.
PR1552.W33Y4 271'.1'0924 79-10546
ISBN 0-8020-5464-1

---

contents

toronto old english series

1 *Computers and Old English Concordances* edited by Angus Cameron, Roberta Frank, and John Leyerle
2 *A Plan for the Dictionary of Old English* edited by Roberta Frank and Angus Cameron
3 *The Stowe Psalter* edited by Andrew C. Kimmens
4 *The Two Versions of Wærferth's Translation of Gregory's Dialogues: An Old English Thesaurus* David Yerkes

general editor's preface

The Toronto Old English Series (TOES) came into being as a response to the needs of the editors of the Dictionary of Old English (DOE), and has three specific aims. The first is to publish Old English texts not yet in print, in order to provide quotable citations for the Dictionary. The second is to replace existing editions whose treatment of the text is unsatisfactory for dictionary use. The third is to provide bibliographical works, semantic studies, and other tools useful for the Dictionary.

The present volume fits into the third category. Bishop Wærferth of Worcester translated the *Dialogues* of Pope Gregory the Great around the year 890; between 950 and 1050 an anonymous reviser compared Wærferth's translation with the Latin and made thousands of (mostly) minor modifications. David Yerkes has listed the differences in vocabulary between the two versions of the translation; the resulting 'thesaurus' is intended as a tool to help us analyse these differences and find reasons for them.

The General Editor would like to express her thanks to the Editorial Board of the series, and to Angus Cameron, Editor of the Dictionary of Old English, who has given unfailing support and guidance and made available all the resources of the DOE project.

This book has been printed by photo-offset lithography from camera-ready copy typed on an IBM Composer by Anna Burko. Her painstaking craftsmanship is apparent on every page.

R.F.
May 1979

bibliography

Alexander, Jonathan J. G. *Anglo-Saxon Illumination in Oxford Libraries* (Oxford 1970)

Ångström, Margareta. *Studies in Old English MSS* (Uppsala diss. 1937)

Asser. *Asser's Life of King Alfred,* ed. William H. Stevenson (Oxford 1904; new impression, with an article on 'Recent Work on Asser's *Life of Alfred*' by Dorothy Whitelock, 1959)

Atkins, Ivor A. and Neil R. Ker. *Catalogus librorum manuscriptorum bibliothecae Wigorniensis: Made in 1622-1623 by Patrick Young* (Cambridge 1944)

Bannister, Henry M. 'Bishop Roger of Worcester and the Church of Keynsham, with a List of Vestments and Books Possibly Belonging to Worcester,' *English Historical Review* 32 (1917) 387-93

Bergmann, Rolf. *Verzeichnis der althochdeutschen und altsächsischen Glossenhandschriften* (Berlin 1973)

Billanovich, Giuseppe. 'Biblioteche di dotti e letteratura italiana tra il Trecento e il Quattrocento,' in *Studi e problemi di critica testuale* (Bologna 1961) pp. 335-48

Bischoff, Bernhard. *Die südostdeutschen Schreibschulen und Bibliotheken in der Karolingerzeit,* vol. 1 (Leipzig 1940; repr. Wiesbaden 1960)

———. *Mittelalterliche Studien,* 2 vols. (Stuttgart 1966-7)

Bischoff, Bernhard and Josef Hofmann. *Libri Sancti Kyliani: Die Würzburger Schreibschule und die Dombibliothek im VIII. und IX. Jahrhundert* (Würzburg 1952)

Bishop, T[erence] A. M. *English Caroline Minuscule* (Oxford 1971)

Bolland, John [Johannes Bollandus] et al., eds. 'Vita [S. Benedicti], auctore S. Gregorio Magno,' in *Acta Sanctorum ... Martii,* vol. 3 (Antwerp 1668) pp. 276-87

Bosworth, Joseph and T[homas] Northcote Toller. *An Anglo-Saxon Dictionary* (Oxford 1882-98); *Supplement* by T. Northcote Toller (Oxford 1908-21; repr. with revised and enlarged addenda by A. Campbell 1972). See also Campbell, Alistair, *Addenda.*

Brunner, Karl. *Altenglische Grammatik nach der angelsächsischen Grammatik von Eduard Sievers,* 3rd ed. (Tübingen 1965)

Bülbring, Karl. Review of *Bischofs Wærferth von Worcester Übersetzung der* Dialoge *Gregors des Grossen,* ed. Hans Hecht, in *Englische Studien* 35 (1905) 100-1

Campbell, Alistair. *Enlarged Addenda and Corrigenda* to the *Anglo-Saxon Dictionary Supplement* by T. Northcote Toller (Oxford 1972)

———. *Old English Grammar* (Oxford 1959)

Campbell, Jackson J. 'The Dialect Vocabulary of the OE Bede,' *Journal of English and Germanic Philology* 50 (1951) 349-72

Clark Hall, J[ohn] R. *A Concise Anglo-Saxon Dictionary,* 4th ed., with a supplement by Herbert D. Meritt (Cambridge 1960)

Cloran, Timothy. *The* Dialogues *of Gregory the Great Translated into Anglo-Norman French by Angier* (Strassburg diss. 1901)

Coxe, Henry O. *Catalogi codicum manuscriptorum bibliothecæ Bodleianæ: Pars tertia, codices Græcos et Latinos Canonicianos* (Oxford 1854)

Cozza-Luzi, Giuseppe, ed. *Historia S. P. N. Benedicti a SS. Pontificibus Romanis Gregorio I descripta* (Tusculanum 1880)

De Nuce, Angelo, ed. *Vita et miracula venerabilis Benedicti,* in *Chronica sacri monasterii Casinensis* by Leo, Marsicanus, Cardinal Bishop of Ostia (Paris 1668) pp. 1-78; repr. in *Rerum Italicarum scriptores,* ed. Ludovico Muratori, vol. 4 (Milan 1723) pp. 151-239

De Vogüé, Adalbert. 'Sur le texte des *Dialogues* de saint Grégoire le Grand: L'utilisation du manuscrit de Milan par les éditeurs,' in *Latinität und alte Kirche: Festschrift für Rudolf Hanslik,* ed. W. Kraus, A. Primmer, and H. Schwabl (Vienna 1977) pp. 326-35

Dufner, Georg. *Die* Dialoge *Gregors des Grossen im Wandel der Zeiten und Sprachen* (Padua 1968)

Einenkel, Eugen. 'Die Englische Verbalnegation,' *Anglia* 35 (1912) 187-248 and 401-24

Engelbert, Pius. 'Die Herkunft des *Ordo regularis*,' *Revue Bénédictine* 77 (1967) 264-97

———. 'Zur Frühgeschichte des Bobbieser Skriptoriums,' *Revue Bénédictine* 78 (1968) 220-60

Förster, Max. Review of *Bischofs Wærferth von Worcester Übersetzung der* Dialoge *Gregors des Grossen*, ed. Hans Hecht, in *Beiblatt zur Anglia* 12 (1901) 97-103 and 169

Funke, Otto. 'Altenglische Wortgeographie,' in *Anglistische Studien: Festschrift zum 70. Geburtstag von Professor Friedrich Wild*, ed. Karl Brunner, Herbert Koziol, and Siegfried Korninger, Wiener Beiträge zur englischen Philologie 66 (Vienna 1958) pp. 39-51

Gallicciolli, Johanne Baptista, ed. *Sancti Gregorii Papæ I, cognomento Magni, opera omnia*, vol. 6 (Venice 1769)

Gneuss, Helmut. *Hymnar und Hymnen im englischen Mittelalter* (Tübingen 1968)

———. 'The Origin of Standard Old English and Æthelwold's School at Winchester,' *Anglo-Saxon England* 1 (1972) 63-83

Gregory the Great. *Opera*, publ. in 1 vol. (Paris 1518); in 2 vols. (Paris 1571); 6 vols. (Rome 1588-93); 6 vols. (Paris 1605); 3 vols. (Paris 1675)

Hart, C[yril J.] R. *The Early Charters of Northern England and the North Midlands* (Leicester 1975)

Harting, P[ieter] N. U. 'The Text of the Old English Translation of Gregory's *Dialogues*,' *Neophilologus* 22 (1937) 281-302

Hecht, Hans, ed. *Bischofs Wærferth von Worcester Übersetzung der* Dialoge *Gregors des Grossen*, Bibliothek der angelsächsischen Prosa 5 (Leipzig 1900; repr. [without pp. 351-74, containing lists of the MS accents] Darmstadt 1965)

———. *Bischof Wærferths von Worcester Übersetzung der* Dialoge *Gregors des Grossen: Einleitung*, Bibliothek der angelsächsischen Prosa 5, part 2 (Hamburg 1907; repr. Darmstadt 1965)

———. *Die Sprache der altenglischen* Dialoge *Gregors des Grossen* (Berlin diss. 1900)

———. 'Zwei Notizen zu den *Dialogen* Gregors in England, 1: Zur Wortdoppelung in der altenglischen Übersetzung der *Dialoge*,' *Englische Studien* 39 (1908) 152-3

Hofmann, Josef. 'Altenglische und althochdeutsche Glossen aus Würzburg und dem weiteren angelsächsischen Missionsgebiet,' *Beiträge zur Geschichte der deutschen Sprache und Literatur* 85 (1963) 27-131

James, Thomas. *Vindiciae Gregorianae* (Geneva 1625)

Johnson, Henry. *Gab es zwei von einander unabhängige altenglische Übersetzungen der* Dialoge *Gregors?* (Berlin diss. 1884)

———. Chase-Johnson Papers (Bowdoin College Library, Brunswick, Maine). Transcript made in November 1882 through January 1883 of British Library, MS. Cotton Otho C.i, vol. 2, fols. 1-137, with many variants recorded from Corpus Christi College, Cambridge, MS. 322.

Jones, Leslie W. 'Ancient Prickings in Eighth-Century Manuscripts,' *Scriptorium* 15 (1961) 14-22

Jordan, Richard. *Eigentümlichkeiten des anglischen Wortschatzes*, Anglistische Forschungen 17 (Heidelberg 1906)

Jost, Karl. *Wulfstanstudien* (Bern 1950)

Kauffmann, Claus M. *Romanesque Manuscripts 1066-1190*, Survey of Manuscripts Illuminated in the British Isles 3 (London 1975)

Keller, Wolfgang. *Zur Litteratur und Sprache von Worcester im X. und XI. Jahrhundert*, 2 vols. (Strassburg diss. 1897, Leipzig 1898; repr. with additions in *Die litterarischen Bestrebungen von Worcester in angelsächsischer Zeit*, Quellen und Forschungen zur Sprach- und Cultur-

geschichte der germanischen Völker 84 [Strassburg 1900])
Ker, Neil R. *Catalogue of Manuscripts Containing Anglo-Saxon* (Oxford 1957)
———. *English Manuscripts in the Century after the Norman Conquest* (Oxford 1960)
———. *Medieval Libraries of Great Britain: A List of Surviving Books,* 2nd ed. (London 1964)
———. *Medieval Manuscripts in British Libraries,* II: *Abbotsford-Keele* (Oxford 1977)
———. 'Salisbury Cathedral Manuscripts and Patrick Young's *Catalogue*,' *Wiltshire Archaeological and Natural History Magazine* 53 (1949) 153-83
———. 'Thomas James's Collation of Gregory, Cyprian, and Ambrose,' *Bodleian Library Record* 4 (1952) 16-30
Klaeber, Friedrich. 'Zur altenglischen Bedaübersetzung,' *Anglia* 25 (1902) 257-315; 27 (1904) 243-82 and 399-435
Krebs, Heinrich. 'Die angelsächsische Übersetzung der *Dialoge* Gregors,' *Anglia* 2 (1879) 65-70
———. 'Zur angelsaechsischen Uebersetzung der *Dialoge* Gregor's,' *Anglia* 3 (1880) 70-73
Liebermann, Felix. 'Zum Urkundenwesen bei den Angelsachsen,' 'Vorrang rechter Seite,' 'Mancus als Goldmünze,' and 'Emendation zu Wærferð,' *Archiv für das Studium der neueren Sprachen* 131 (1913) 153
Lowe, Elias A. *The Beneventan Script* (Oxford 1914)
———. *Codices Latini antiquiores,* 11 vols. and *Supplement* (Oxford 1934-71)
———. *Palaeographical Papers, 1907-1965,* ed. Ludwig Bieler, 2 vols. (Oxford 1972)
Loyn, Henry R. 'The Term *ealdorman* in the Translations Prepared at the Time of King Alfred,' *English Historical Review* 68 (1953) 513-25
Mabillon, Jean, ed. 'Vita S. Benedicti ... ex Gregorio Magno in toto lib. 2 Dialog,' in *Acta Sanctorum ordinis S. Benedicti,* vol. 1 (Paris 1668) pp. 3-28
Maurists [monachorum Ordinis Sancti Benedicti, e Congregatione Sancti Mauri], eds. *Sancti Gregorii Papæ I, cognomento Magni, opera omnia,* vol. 2 (Paris 1705)
Mayer, Hartwig. 'Bericht über das Vorhaben einer Edition bisher ungedruckter althochdeutscher Glossen,' *Frühmittelalterliche Studien* 7 (1973) 228-33
Menner, Robert J. 'Anglian and Saxon Elements in Wulfstan's Vocabulary,' *Modern Language Notes* 63 (1948) 1-9
———. 'The Anglian Vocabulary of the *Blickling Homilies*,' in *Philologica: The Malone Anniversary Studies,* ed. Thomas A. Kirby and Henry Bosley Woolf (Baltimore 1949) pp. 56-64
———. 'The Vocabulary of the Old English Poems on Judgment Day,' *PMLA* 62 (1947) 583-97
Meritt, Herbert D. *Old English Glosses* (New York 1945)
Migne, Jacques Paul, ed. Patrologiæ cursus completus ... series Latina, vol. 66 (Paris 1847) cols. 125-204 [Bk. II of Gregory's *Dialogues*]; and vol. 77 (Paris 1849) cols. 149-430 [Bks. I, III, and IV]
Mittermüller, Rupert, ed. *S. Gregorii Magni dialogorum liber secundus de vita ... S. Benedicti* (Ratisbon 1880)
Moricca, Umberto, ed. *Gregorii Magni dialogi libri IV,* Fonti per la Storia d'Italia (Rome 1924)
Omont, Henri. *Catalogue général des manuscrits des bibliothèques publiques de France, Départements: Tome premier, Rouen,* vol. 1 (Paris 1886)
Orengo, Renato. *Le* Dialogue *de saint Gregoire le Grand traduit par Angier* (Zurich 1969)
Pächt, Otto and Jonathan J. G. Alexander. *Illuminated Manuscripts in the Bodleian Library, Oxford,* 3 vols. (Oxford 1966-73)
Potter, Simeon. 'On the Relation of the Old English Bede to Werferth's Gregory and to Alfred's Translations,' in *Mémoires de la Société Royale des Sciences de Bohême, 1930* (Prague 1931)

Quirini, Angelo M. *Vita Latino-Græca S. P. Benedicti* (Venice 1723)
Rauh, Hildegard. *Der Wortschatz der altenglischen Uebersetzungen des Matthaeus-Evangeliums untersucht auf seine dialektische und zeitliche Gebundenheit* (Berlin diss. 1936)
Robertson, Agnes J. *Anglo-Saxon Charters* (Cambridge 1939; repr. 1956)
Rose, Valentin. *Verzeichniss der lateinischen Handschriften der Königlichen Bibliothek zu Berlin,* vol. 2 (Berlin 1901)
Schabram, Hans. *Superbia: Studien zum altenglischen Wortschatz,* vol. 1 (Munich 1965)
Scherer, Günther. *Zur Geographie und Chronologie des angelsächsischen Wortschatzes, im Anschluss an Bischof Wærferth's Übersetzung der* Dialoge *Gregors* (Berlin diss. 1928)
S[chulze], W[ilhelm]. 'Zur Blattfüllung: Ags. *nǽnigra (nánra) þinga,' Zeitschrift für vergleichende Sprachforschung* 60 (1932-3) 144
Seebold, Elmar. 'Die ae. Entsprechungen von lat. *sapiens* und *prudens,' Anglia* 92 (1974) 291-333
Sepulcri, Alessandro. 'Le alterazioni fonetiche e morfologiche nel latino di Gregorio Magno e del suo tempo,' *Studi Medievali* 1 (1904) 171-234
Sievers, Eduard: see Brunner, Karl
Sisam, Kenneth. 'A Gloss to Gregory's *Dialogues,' Review of English Studies* 2 (1951) 48
———. 'An Old English Translation of a Letter from Wynfrith to Eadburga (A.D. 716-17) in Cotton MS. Otho C.i' [repr. from *Modern Language Review* 18 (1923) 253-72] and 'Addendum: The Verses Prefixed to Gregory's *Dialogues*,' in *Studies in the History of Old English Literature* (Oxford 1953) pp. 199-231
Steinmeyer, Elias [Emil Elias von] and Eduard Sievers, eds. *Die althochdeutschen Glossen,* vol. 2 (Berlin 1882)
Temple, Elżbieta. *Anglo-Saxon Manuscripts 900-1066,* Survey of Manuscripts Illuminated in the British Isles 2 (London 1976)
Thoma, Herbert. 'Altdeutsches aus Vatikanischen und Münchener Handschriften,' *Beiträge zur Geschichte der deutschen Sprache und Literatur* 85 (1963) 220-47
Tilley, Morris P. *Zur Syntax Wærferths* (Leipzig diss. 1903)
Timmer, Benno J. 'The Place of the Attributive Noun-Genitive in Anglo-Saxon,' *English Studies* 21 (1939) 49-72
———. *Studies in Bishop Wærferth's Translation of the* Dialogues *of Gregory the Great* (Wageningen 1934)
Vleeskruyer, Rudolf. *The Life of St. Chad: An Old English Homily* (Amsterdam 1953)
Waitz, Georg, ed. *Ex Gregorii Magni dialogorum libris,* Monumenta Germaniae historica: Scriptores rerum Langobardicarum et Italicarum saec. VI-IX (Hannover 1878) pp. 524-40
Wanley, Humphrey. *Antiquæ literaturæ septentrionalis ... qui in Angliæ bibliothecis extant,* in *Linguarum vett. septentrionalium thesaurus grammatico-criticus et archæologicus* by George Hickes, vol. 2 (Oxford 1705)
Wenisch, Franz. 'Kritische Bemerkungen zun Angaben über die Verbreitung einiger angeblich westsächsischen Dialektwörter,' *Anglia* 96 (1978) 5-44
William of Malmesbury. *Willelmi Malmesbiriensis monachi de gestis regum Anglorum,* ed. William Stubbs, Rolls Series 90, vol. 1 (London 1887)
Yerkes, David. 'The Chapter Titles of Book I of Gregory's *Dialogues,' Revue Bénédictine,* forthcoming 1979
———. 'Dugdale's Dictionary and Somner's *Dictionarium,' English Language Notes* 14 (1976) 110-12
———. 'An Elementary Way to Illuminate Detail of Textual History,' *Manuscripta* 21 (1977) 38-41

———. 'The Medieval Provenance of Corpus Christi College, Cambridge, MS. 322,' *Transactions of the Cambridge Bibliographical Society* 7 (1978) 245-7

———. 'A Neglected Transcript of the Cotton Manuscript of Wærferth's Old English Translation of Gregory's *Dialogues*,' *Neuphilologische Mitteilungen* 79 (1978) 21-2

———. 'A New Collation of MS. Hatton 76, Part 'A',' *Anglia* 94 (1976) 163-5

———. 'A New Collation of the Cambridge Manuscript of the Old English Translation of Gregory's *Dialogues*,' *Mediaevalia* 3 (1977) 165-72

———. 'The Place of Composition of the Opening of Napier Homily I,' *Neophilologus* 60 (1976) 452-4

———. 'The Text of the Canterbury Fragment of Werferth's Translation of Gregory's *Dialogues* and Its Relation to the Other Manuscripts,' *Anglo-Saxon England* 6 (1977) 121-35

———. 'Two Early Manuscripts of Gregory's *Dialogues*,' *Manuscripta* 19 (1975) 171-3

———. 'An Unnoticed Omission in the Modern Critical Editions of Gregory's *Dialogues*,' *Revue Bênédictine* 87 (1977) 178-9

Zimmermann, Ernst H. *Vorkarolingische Miniaturen*, vol. 1 (Berlin 1916)

signs and abbreviations

bk(s).	book(s)
ca.	circa
cf.	'compare'
ch.	chapter
col(s).	column(s)
def.	defective
diss.	dissertation
ed(s).	editor(s), edited by
e.g.	'for example'
esp.	'especially'
fol(s).	folio(s)
HS	Handschrift
i.e.	'namely'
MS(S)	Manuscript(s)
n.	note (footnote)
no.	number
om.	omitted
p(p).	page(s)
pl.	plate
publ.	published
repr.	reprint, reprinted
var.	variant
vol(s).	volume(s)
[...x]	'occurs ... number of times'

manuscript sigla

Old English manuscripts (the sigla *C, H,* and *O* come from Krebs, Johnson, Hecht, and others; the siglum *A* from *Anglo-Saxon England* 6 [1977] 121-35):

A	Canterbury Cathedral, Add. 25
C	Corpus Christi College, Cambridge, 322
H	Bodleian, Hatton 76, fols. 1-54
O	British Library, Cotton Otho C.i, vol. 2, fols. 1-137

Latin manuscripts (the sigla *A, C, M,* O_1, O_2, *S,* V_1, V_2, V_3, and V_4 come from Moricca; *Cl, La, Ro, Sa,* and *Ta* from *Neophilologus* 60 [1976] 452-4; and W_1 and W_2 from *Manuscripta* 19 [1975] 171-3):

A	Milan, Ambrosiana B.159 Sup.
Be_1	Berlin, Deutsche Staatsbibliothek, Theol. Lat. Fol. 432
Be_2	Berlin, Deutsche Staatsbibliothek, Theol. Lat. Fol. 466
Bo	Bodley 190
C	Monte Cassino, Archivio della Badia 85
Cl	Clare College, Cambridge, 30
Hf	Hereford Cathedral O.i.10
La	Lambeth Palace 204
M	Verona, Biblioteca Capitolare XLVI (44)
Mu	Munich, Bayrische Staatsbibliothek Clm. 2944
O_1	Rome, Vallicelliana C.9, fols. 174-81 and 186-275
O_2	Rome, Vallicelliana C.9, fols. 1-137
Pa_1	Bodleian, Canon. Pat. Lat. 166
Pa_2	Bodleian, Canon. Pat. Lat. 105
Ro	Rouen, Bibliothèque Municipale A.337 (506)
S	Rome, Biblioteca Nazionale, Sessoriana 40 (1258)
Sa	Salisbury Cathedral 96
St_1	St. Gall, Stiftsbibliothek 213
St_2	St. Gall, Stiftsbibliothek 214
St_3	St. Gall, Stiftsbibliothek 215
Ta	Bodleian, Tanner 3
V_1	Vatican, Palat. Lat. 260
V_2	Vatican, Palat. Lat. 261
V_3	Vatican, Palat. Lat. 262
V_4	Vatican, Vatic. Lat. 5753
W_1	Wrocław, Biblioteka Uniwersytecka, Akc. 1955/2 and 1969/430
W_2	Würzburg Universitätsbibliothek, M. P. Theol. Fol. 19

introduction

At King Alfred's command, in the last quarter of the ninth century Bishop Wærferth of Worcester translated Gregory's *Dialogues* into English. About a century or a century and a half later, between 950 and 1050, someone, again perhaps working at Worcester, carefully compared the translation with the Latin and revised the translation accordingly.[1] The anonymous reviser changed thousands of words and phrases, sometimes no doubt to render the Latin more closely, at other times apparently only to bring the diction of the translation up to date or into conformity with that of his own dialect. On occasion, however, none of these explanations seems to apply. For instance, to translate *famulus* the reviser twice substituted *þeow* for *wer,* once *wer* for *þeow.* The pair may represent true synonyms – an Old English counterpart to Fowler's 'gorse' and 'furze'; more likely, the reviser sensed some crucial difference in the context. Whatever the reasons for the new words, when put alongside the old words of the original translation they form a sizable and unique Old English thesaurus.

Wærferth's original translation survives in two manuscripts, Corpus Christi College, Cambridge, 322 (Ker 60), '*C,*' and British Library, Cotton Otho C.i, vol. 2, fols. 1-137 (Ker 182), '*O.*' The fragment of another manuscript of Wærferth's translation, Canterbury Cathedral, Add. 25 (Ker 96; '*A*'), contains a small part of the fourth, and last, book of the *Dialogues.* Since the revision survives in a single manuscript, Bodleian, Hatton 76, fols. 1-54 (Ker 328), '*H,*' that contains only a little over two-thirds of Books I and II, *A* and *H* never coincide. *C* and *H,* both written in the eleventh century, quite possibly at Worcester, also share a prefatory letter by King Alfred not found in *O.* A scribe, perhaps in the Southwest, copied the first two books of the translation in *O* at the beginning of the eleventh century; another scribe copied the last two books at Worcester about forty years later, in the middle of the century.[2] Hecht drew two possible stemmata to represent the genetic relation among *C, O,* and *H.* With either stemma the agreement of *C* and *O* establishes the reading of an exemplar of Wærferth's original translation from which the revision in *H* descends. Sisam discredited the stemmata, but none of his arguments would give any additional authority to *H*'s readings. *CO* still witnesses either the actual copy of the translation used by the reviser or an ancestor of the reviser's copy.[3]

Of the two previous studies on the vocabulary of the translation, Scherer's is worthless and Hecht's (*Einleitung,* pp. 134-83) incomplete. Harting showed that Scherer worked from Hecht

1 Asser (ch. 77; p. 62) and William of Malmesbury (bk. 2, §122; p. 131) record Alfred's command. Æthelred consecrated Wærferth to the see of Worcester in 872 or 873 (Hart, pp. 363-4). For the date and place of composition of the revision, see Keller, *Die litterarischen Bestrebungen,* p. 66; Hecht, *Einleitung,* pp. 26-7; and Sisam, *Studies,* p. 229. The date of the unique manuscript, Hatton 76, provides the *terminus ad quem* (see below). Potter discussed 'the points of relationship' between the revision and the original translation, including vocabulary (pp. 35-40).

2 The manuscript dates are Ker's, who assigned *H* to the first half of the century, *C* to the second half. The 'tremulous' hand of Worcester glossed *H* in the first half of the thirteenth century, and an even earlier Worcester reader glossed *C* in the twelfth century (see the description below of Clare College, Cambridge, MS. 30 [*Cl*]). Ångström argued at length that a Bury St. Edmunds librarian catalogued *C,* probably in the fifteenth century, but Ker rejected that provenance (*Medieval Libraries,* p. 22). The entry '.II. englissce dialogas' (Robertson, p. 250) in the mid-eleventh-century booklist found in Corpus Christi College, Cambridge, MS. 367 may place *H* and *O* at Worcester (Ker, *Catalogue,* MS. 64). Ker believed that a Worcester scribe wrote the second part of *O* in the middle of the eleventh century, and the 'tremulous' hand later glossed both parts of the manuscript (*Catalogue,* MS. 182). The 'regular alternation of the colours red, blue, and green' in its initials suggests, however, that the first part of *O* originated at Exeter (Ker, *Catalogue,* p. xxxviii). Sisam attributed *O*'s metrical preface, but not the few lines of prose that follow, to Wulfsige, Bishop of Sherborne in Alfred's time (*Studies,* pp. 201-3 and 225-31, esp. 229 n.). A diplomatic text of the fragment *A,* discovered fifty years after the time of Hecht's edition, appears in *Anglo-Saxon England* 6 (1977) 121-35.

3 *Einleitung,* pp. 29-35; *Studies,* p. 229 and n.

and Bosworth-Toller rather than from the text itself, usually with misleading, if not ludicrous, results. Hecht provided wordlists much in the manner of the present study, but he chose to include far fewer entries and did not give all the citations. To show that the revision does indeed represent a reworking of Wærferth, and not a second, independent translation, Johnson compiled what could be regarded as a complement to a thesaurus. He listed many of the words and phrases *shared* by the two versions of the translation. Five textual or syntactic studies of Wærferth's translation include some lexicographic material. Hecht (*Einleitung,* pp. 36-121; see also Hecht's 'Zwei Notizen'), Tilley, and Harting focused almost exclusively on the original translation, but Potter and, notably, Timmer (*Studies*) treated the revision as well. Liebermann and Schulze have contributed minor textual notes; and many studies of particular words or word groups or of the vocabulary of other Old English works cite examples from the translation, though the examples often come from Scherer's monograph rather than from the text itself: e.g. the studies by Klaeber, Jordan, Einenkel, Rauh, Timmer ('Place of the Attributive'), Menner, Jost (pp. 158-62 and 184-7), J. Campbell, Loyn (pp. 519-21), Vleeskruyer (pp. 23-37), Funke, Schabram (pp. 42-5), Gneuss (*Hymnar und Hymnen,* pp. 173-90), Seebold (pp. 297-8), and Wenisch. Confirming Hecht's observation (*Einleitung,* p. 131), Gneuss has recently indicated the 'close and remarkable' correspondences of vocabulary between 'the Winchester group' – products of Æthelwold's school – and the revision of Wærferth's translation ('Origin of Standard Old English,' p. 81).

The thesaurus lists all the differences in vocabulary between the two versions of the translation, when the reading of *H* differs from the reading of both *C* and *O* (*C* and *O* may or may not themselves agree). When *H* differs from one of the manuscripts, *C* or *O,* but agrees with the other, it is assumed that the reviser (witnessed by *H*) took the reading from his copy of the original translation (witnessed in this instance by whichever manuscript, *C* or *O,* agrees with *H*). *C* and *O* have equal weight in the thesaurus; the reading of each always appears in full in every entry.

The Latin, whenever it corresponds to the Old English words or phrases of the entry, follows immediately. The three printed critical editions of all or selected parts of the *Dialogues,* and twelve manuscripts collated independently by the present writer provide the Latin text and variants.[4] The manuscripts include the only five thought to have been written in England before 1100 (*Cl, La, Ro, Ta,* and W_1)[5] and seven others, all from the beginning of the twelfth century or earlier. The Maurists (1705) and Moricca (1924) printed all of the *Dialogues;* Waitz (1878) printed selections from each of the four books. In the accompanying brief descriptions of the twelve manuscripts collated independently, page and line numbers refer to Moricca's edition:

4 *Hf, Ro,* St_1, W_1, and W_2 were collated from microfilms, the other seven from the manuscripts themselves. Hecht's wordlists include the Latin, but only the reading of the Maurists' edition (*Einleitung,* pp. I-II). Six critical editions of Book II, the life of Benedict, have not been collated for the present study: those of Bolland, De Nuce, and Mabillon (all 1668), Quirini (1723), and Cozza-Luzi and Mittermüller (both 1880). Bolland and Mabillon did not list the sources for their texts, but both editions were in turn used by the Maurists (p. 117). De Nuce based his text on Monte Cassino, Archivio della Badia MS. 85 (*C*), a witness subsequently collated by Moricca and Waitz; and Quirini used two 'MSS. Subiacensibus.' Cozza-Luzi, like Moricca and Waitz, based his text on the eighth-century Milan, Ambrosiana MS. B.159 Sup. (*A*) (see De Vogüé, pp. 326-7); and Mittermüller based his on Munich, Bayrische Staatsbibliothek HS. Clm. 22038.

5 Though not written in England, Salisbury Cathedral MS. 96 (*Sa*) may have arrived there before 1100 (see below). Canterbury Cathedral, Add. MS. 32, the fragment of a single leaf from Book III, has two Old English glosses, each of which agrees almost exactly with the corresponding reading of Wærferth's translation (see *Anglo-Saxon England* 6 [1977] 130, n. 2). Ker dated the Latin and the glosses to the beginning of the eleventh century. He identified the glossator's hand as English but did not assign a place for the original script (*Catalogue,* MS. 97*, p. lxiii; see also *Medieval Manuscripts,* p. 315). For all seven manuscripts – *Cl, La, Ro, Ta,* W_1, *Sa,* and the Canterbury fragment – see further *Neophilologus* 60 (1976) 452-4.

Bo Bodley 190. Written in England at the beginning of the twelfth century, with a thirteenth-century provenance of Exeter (Pächt and Alexander, vol. 3, MS. 81). By collating *Bo* and three other English manuscripts (Bodleian, Auct. D.2.7, and Bodley 230 and 688), Bodley's first librarian, Thomas James, corrected thirty-eight corrupt passages in the text of the *Dialogues* found in the Rome 1588-93 edition of Gregory's complete works (James, pp. 86-90).[6] None of the readings James published from the manuscripts was of any use in the present study.

Cl Clare College, Cambridge, 30. Written perhaps at Worcester (Bishop, p. 20 n.) 'either a little before or a little after the Conquest' (Ker, *English Manuscripts,* p. 8, n. 2). Kauffmann assigned five decorated initials in the manuscript to the late eleventh century and Worcester (MS. 4). Like *O* and *H* of the Old English translation, *Cl* was glossed in the first half of the thirteenth century by the 'tremulous' hand of Worcester (Ker, *Medieval Libraries,* pp. 206, 207, and 209). A third witness of the translation, *C,* has several twelfth-century Latin glosses copied from the text of *Cl* (see *Transactions of the Cambridge Bibliographical Society* 7 [1978] 245-7).

Hf Hereford Cathedral O.i.10. Written at the beginning of the twelfth century, with a medieval provenance of Cirencester (Ker, *Medieval Libraries,* p. 51).

La Lambeth Palace 204. Written at the beginning of the eleventh century (Ker, *Catalogue,* MS. 277), perhaps at Christ Church, Canterbury (Bishop, p. xvi, n. 2; see also Temple, MS. 19(x)). *La* has four Old English glosses, dated by Ker to the middle of the eleventh century and printed by Meritt (no. 17; see also Sisam, 'A Gloss'). The glosses differ completely from the readings of Wærferth's translation.

Pa_1 Bodleian, Canon. Pat. Lat. 166. Missing leaves at 16.5 *oritur*-16.25 and 24.7 *ad*-25.13 *narrabat,* with replacement leaves in a later hand at 35.5 *ei*-59.3 *acceperat.* Written in Italy in the second half of the eleventh century (Pächt and Alexander, vol. 2, MS. 16) and (the replacement leaves) at the end of the fourteenth century (Coxe, col. 387).

Pa_2 Bodleian, Canon. Pat. Lat. 105. Written in the first half of the twelfth century in northern Italy, perhaps Emilia (Pächt and Alexander, vol. 2, MS. 36).

Ro Rouen, Bibliothèque Municipale A.337 (506). Missing many leaves, including all of Book I; begins at 99.10 *numquid.* Written in the tenth century (Omont, p. 111), perhaps at Christ Church, Canterbury (Bishop, pp. xxv-xxvi).

Sa Salisbury Cathedral 96. Badly injured by damp, begins at 42.7 *ita* and wants a leaf at 53.1 *quod*-54.23 *violentus.* Written in a Continental hand perhaps in the tenth century (Neil R. Ker's note in the 'Census of Books from English Medieval Libraries,' kept in Duke Humphrey's library at the Bodleian), with a 1622 provenance of Salisbury (Ker, 'Salisbury Manuscripts,' p. 168, where the date of the manuscript is given as the tenth century without question). For an inconclusive indication of earlier English provenance, see Ker, *English Manuscripts,* p. 49.

St_1 St. Gall, Stiftsbibliothek 213. Written in the middle of the eighth century in pre-Caroline minuscule, probably at St. Gall (Lowe, vol. 7, MS. 922, who added that 'the script on part of p. 173 is in manifest imitation of Insular majuscule').

Ta Bodleian, Tanner 3. Written during the second quarter of the eleventh century, with a twelfth-century provenance (on the basis of a letter) of Worcester (Pächt and Alexander, vol. 3, MS. 45). Bishop tentatively assigned the script to Worcester (p. 20 n.), but Temple likened the contemporary frontispiece, on fol. 1v, to Winchester productions (MS. 89). Alexander dated the manuscript to the first quarter of the eleventh century (p. 11), and

6 Ker has given a full account of James's work ('Thomas James's Collation').

Ker dated it to the beginning of the eleventh century and questioned a Worcester provenance (*Medieval Libraries,* p. 209; *English Manuscripts,* p. 20, n. 4). The back of the last leaf of the text of the *Dialogues* (fol. 189v) contains, in a hand of about 1100 (Ker, *Medieval Libraries,* p. 205), a list of books that may have belonged to Worcester (see Bannister, pp. 388-9, and Atkins and Ker, p. 1 n.).

W_1 Wrocław, Biblioteka Uniwersytecka, Akc. 1955/2 and 1969/430 (formerly 'Fragm. R.1'). Seven damaged bifolia containing 81.21-83.17, 93.17-96.20, 131.8-133.8, 144.17-146.19, 149.12-151.6, 162.14-165.2, and 167.1-182.25. Written about the year 700 in a Northumbrian hand, with tenth-century corrections in a Continental hand (Lowe, vol. 11, MS. 1595, and *Supplement,* p. 31). See also Bischoff, *Studien,* vol. 2, p. 339. The text of the *Dialogues* in W_1 is an ancestor of that in W_2 (see *Manuscripta* 19 [1975] 171-3 and *Revue Bénédictine* 87 [1977] 178-9).

W_2 Würzburg, Universitätsbibliothek, M. P. Theol. Fol. 19. Two leaves are missing at 87.3 *proprium*-90.16 *illius.* Written about the year 800 in Caroline and Anglo-Saxon minuscule at a West German scriptorium, perhaps Lorsch (Lowe, vol. 9, MS. 1406), with a ca.800 provenance of Würzburg (Lowe, *Papers,* vol. 1, pp. 242-3); contains a few Old High German glosses (see most recently Hofmann, pp. 73-4). See also Bischoff and Hofmann, pp. 59, 105, and 143. W_2's text of the *Dialogues* descends from that of W_1 (see above).

The Latin manuscripts *Cl* and *Hf* share one particularly strong tie with the Old English manuscript, *H,* of the revision of Wærferth's translation: all three have 35 chapter titles for Book I. Of the other ten Latin manuscripts just described, *Bo,* Pa_1, and St_1 do not have any chapter titles; Pa_2, *Ta,* and W_2 have the standard 12 printed by Moricca, the Maurists, and others. The surviving parts of *Ro* and W_1 do not include Book I, and *Sa* has some of the numbers in the text for the 12-chapter division but no titles (though the leaves lost from the beginning of the manuscript may have contained a table of contents with titles). Thirty-five chapter titles for Book I found in *La* do not correspond to those of *Cl* and *Hf.* Wærferth's original translation, in the Old English Canterbury fragment (*A*), as well as in manuscripts *C* and *O,* does not include any titles. *C* has the illuminated numbers *IIII* and *VIII* at the places in Book I appropriate for the 12-chapter division (Hecht 26.3 and 51.32, respectively); *O*'s syntax bridges the former chapter break, however (at 26.3), and elsewhere the syntax of both *C* and *O* does so, e.g. at 9.19-11.3 *ic geleornode 7 gefrægn æt gesægene swiðe arwyrðra witena þæt ic nu secge, þæt hit gelamp geo in Samni þære mægðe þæt …* (Hecht's edition misreports *O*'s text at the crucial place, *þæt ic nu secge, þæt; O* actually reads the same as *C*). Thirteen other Latin manuscripts of the *Dialogues,* all probably written in England or (perhaps in one instance) copied from an English manuscript, share the 35 chapter titles found in *Cl* and *Hf.*[7] The two oldest witnesses of the titles – Old English manuscript *H* and Latin manuscript *Cl* – both come from Worcester.

Until Dom Adalbert de Vogüé publishes his edition of the *Dialogues* in the *Sources chrétiennes,*

7 MSS. Blickling Hall, Aylsham, Norfolk, 6864; Cambridge University Library Ee.5.32; British Library Burney 320, Royal 7.E.i, and Royal 8.F.xiv; Bodleian Auct. D.2.7, Bodley 688, and Rawlinson C.34; Jesus College, Oxford, 41 and 42; New College, Oxford, 140; University College, Oxford, 6; and Rouen, Bibliothèque Municipale A.324 (509). Pembroke College, Cambridge, MS. 230 numbers 35 chapters at the appropriate places in the text but does not have any titles. The Rouen manuscript once stood next on the shelf at Jumièges to our *Ro,* another copy of the *Dialogues,* thought to have been written at Christ Church, Canterbury (Rouen, Bibliothèque Municipale A.337 (506), described above; see Omont, pp. xix-xxiii, xxxix-xli, and 111-12). The Maurists quote two of the 35 titles in the critical apparatus to their printed edition, probably from Rouen MS. 509 (see p. 117 and cols. 156 and 176). An Anglo-Norman translation of the *Dialogues* completed at Oxford in 1212 or 1213 by 'Angier' has 35 chapter titles (see Cloran, and Orengo, though neither printed the titles). The 35 Latin chapter titles appear in *Revue Bénédictine,* forthcoming 1979.

Moricca's critical edition of 1924 must remain the standard. Moricca collated ten Italian manuscripts of the twelfth century or earlier, basing his text on the eighth-century Milan, Ambrosiana B.159 Sup. (*A*) and giving all important variants from the other nine (pp. LXXXI-XCV). De Vogüé's edition uses most of Moricca's manuscripts and two others, of the eighth century: St. Gall, Stiftsbibliothek 213 (St_1), described above, and Autun, Bibliothèque Municipale 20 (S. 21) (Lowe, vol. 6, MS. 719). Already De Vogüé has published corrections to Moricca's edition, mainly to his text of *A*. In the following descriptions Moricca has provided the sigla and, unless indicated otherwise, the dates:

A Milan, Ambrosiana B.159 Sup. Written at Bobbio in the middle of the eighth century (Lowe, vol. 3, MS. 309) and amended by a ninth- or (Waitz) eleventh-century hand. See Engelbert, 'Zur Frühgeschichte,' for the most recent discussion of this manuscript and its importance.

C Monte Cassino, Archivio della Badia 85. Written in the eleventh century or (Lowe, *Beneventan Script,* p. 299) about 1200.

M Verona, Biblioteca Capitolare XLVI (44). Begins at 23.10. Written at Verona in the first half of the eighth century (Lowe, vol. 4, MS. 503).

O_1 Rome, Vallicelliana C.9, fols. 174-81 and 186-275. Begins at 118.21. Written in the ninth century.

O_2 Rome, Vallicelliana C.9, fols. 1-137. Written in the eleventh or (Lowe, *Beneventan Script,* p. 359) at the beginning of the twelfth century.

S Rome, Biblioteca Nazionale, Sessoriana 40 (1258). Written at Nonantola in the ninth century (Lowe, *Beneventan Script,* p. 114).

V_1 Vatican, Palat. Lat. 260. Written in the tenth century.

V_2 Vatican, Palat. Lat. 261. Written in the ninth and tenth centuries; contains Old High German glosses (Mayer, pp. 230-31).

V_3 Vatican, Palat. Lat. 262. Written in the tenth century. Dufner has briefly discussed an aspect of the manuscript's textual history (p. 105).

V_4 Vatican, Vatic. Lat. 5753. Written in the ninth or (Waitz) tenth century. Billanovich (p. 345) and De Vogüé (p. 332) have referred to this as a Bobbio manuscript.

Moricca showed that *A, C,* O_2, *S,* V_3, and V_4 all descend from an archetype written at Monte Cassino (p. LXXXIV; see most recently Engelbert, 'Die Herkunft,' pp. 280-88).

Waitz printed only selections from the *Dialogues* in his critical edition for the Monumenta Germaniae historica, including seven passages from Books I and II: 20.8 *vir*-22.7, 38.8-39.5, 63.10 *quadam*-63.14 *subiacebat,* 101.3-103.15, 106.21 *vir*-108.10 *custodirit,* 109.3-109.5 *conversa,* and 122.5-122.9 *exirit.* The text comes from *A*, as in Moricca's edition, with variants cited from St_1 (see above), *C* and V_4 (also used by Moricca), and five other manuscripts (pp. 524-5):

Be_1 Berlin, Deutsche Staatsbibliothek, Theol. Lat. Fol. 432. Lacks all but the fourth of the passages printed by Waitz (101.3-103.15). Written in the ninth and tenth centuries, with a provenance of Herford (Rose, p. 105).

Be_2 Berlin, Deutsche Staatsbibliothek, Theol. Lat. Fol. 466. Lacks the first passage printed by Waitz. Written in the eleventh century (Rose, p. 105), with later corrections.

Mu Munich, Bayrische Staatsbibliothek Clm. 2944. Lacks all except the fifth (106.21-108.10) and last of the passages printed by Waitz. Written in the tenth century in southern Germany (Bischoff, *Schreibschulen,* pp. 167-8); contains over a dozen Old High German glosses printed by Steinmeyer and Sievers, vol. 2, p. 262, and Thoma, p. 237.

St_2 St. Gall, Stiftsbibliothek 214. Lacks all except the fourth (101.3-103.15) and last of the passages printed by Waitz. Written in the eighth century, possibly in northeast France (Lowe, vol. 7, MS. 924, where fragments in St. Gall 9, 12, 762, and 942, a lost fragment of St. Paul in Corinthia, and the two fragments Zurich, Zentralbibliothek C.184, Nos. XVII and XVIII are all described as originally part of the same manuscript). Bischoff dated the hand to the second half of the century (*Studien,* vol. 1, p. 10, n. 31; see also Jones, p. 19).

St_3 St. Gall, Stiftsbibliothek 215. Written in the tenth century (Waitz); contains one or two Old High German glosses printed by Steinmeyer and Sievers, vol. 2, p. 259 (see further Bergmann, p. 26).

For his study of the phonology and morphology of the *Dialogues,* Sepulcri quoted a large number of forms from St_2 and St_3, as well as from *A, M,* and St_1, often from passages not used by Waitz. The present study, however, does not draw upon Sepulcri's readings.

For their seminal critical edition of the *Dialogues,* published in 1705 in the second volume of the complete works of Gregory, the Maurists (p. 117) used nineteen French manuscripts and four printed texts (Paris 1518, 1571, 1605, and 1675), the collations of Thomas James (see the description above of Bodley 190 [*Bo*]), and the critical editions of Book II, the life of Benedict, prepared by Bolland and Mabillon (see note 4 above). Unfortunately, the Maurists did not name the authority for their base text (it may be the St. Germain manuscript that heads the list of sources) and gave only a few variants per page. Gallicciolli and Migne, among others, have reprinted the edition. Though he usually cut back the critical apparatus, Gallicciolli also added a handful of readings from three manuscripts not used by the Maurists (p. 34).

Those passages shared by Wærferth's original translation, in manuscripts *C* and *O,* and the revision of the translation, in *H,* form the corpus of the present study (Old English line numbers refer to Hecht, Latin line numbers to Moricca):

	Old English	*Latin*
Alfred's prefatory letter	1.1-21	——
Opening of the translation	2.22-3.1	——
Translation of Book I	3.2-9.22,	13.2-16.25,
	14.24-47.5,	21.3-41.14,
	50.13-90.24	46.8-69.21
Opening of Book II	94.12-26	——
Translation of Book II	94.26-98.8,	71.5-75.4,
	100.24-110.26,	78.21-84.5,
	113.19-118.31,	89.5-92.7,
	123.9-152.25,	97.3-115.4,
	154.8-159.4,	116.11-119.3,
	162.1-164.17,	121.22-123.8,
	169.5-174.23	127.23-131.12

O does not have a copy of Alfred's letter, but all the other passages survive in both *C* and *O.* A metrical preface and a few preliminary lines in prose appear only in *O* (Hecht 2.1-21); tables of contents before each book (9.23-10.40 and 93.1-94.9, respectively), chapter titles in the text (11.1-2, 16.5, 17.1, etc.), and two lines at the start of Book II (94.10-11) appear only in *H.* The loss of leaves from *H* explains the larger gaps in the text proper of Books I and II (11.3-14.24, 47.5-50.12, etc.).

The thesaurus consists of the differences of vocabulary between the two versions of the translation numbered in order as they appear in the text. Asterisks accompany the first seven numbers as a reminder that these entries record the differences between the two manuscripts, *C* and *H,* of Alfred's prefatory letter rather than differences between the two versions of Wærferth's work. All the Old English readings come directly from the manuscripts, but, for convenience, line numbers refer to Hecht's edition, and notes to the thesaurus record all deviations from his text. Hecht printed *C* and *H* in parallel columns, *O*'s variants from *C* in a critical apparatus at the foot of each page. The numbers refer to the line on which the reading of *C* begins; *H*'s corresponding reading usually lies on the same line or nearby. Hecht reported *C* and *H* with remarkable accuracy, though, unhappily, he decided to transcribe ę as *e* instead of reproducing it or substituting *æ* (p. VI; see the reviews by Förster [p. 102] and Bülbring [p. 101], and compare Hecht's policy in his dissertation on the phonology of the short tonic vowels in *C* and *O* [*Sprache*], where he printed ę). The brief list of the important errors in Hecht's text of *C* appears in *Mediaevalia* 3 (1977) 165-72; the list for his *H*, in *Anglia* 94 (1976) 163-5. *O* needs a new editor.

For the thesaurus entries, the Old English readings incorporate corrections made by the original hands, expand abbreviations (except for the tironian nota 7, as well as a few others pointed out in notes), and ignore erasures, corrections or glosses by later hands (except for one or two glosses included with the notes), and manuscript capitalization and word-division. One scribe wrote the text of *C*, which stands free of later corrections and has only a handful of Latin glosses.[8] Two scribes prepared Books I and II of the translation in *O*, the main textual hand and the rubricator, who, besides decorating the manuscript, amended the text in several places. Notes to the thesaurus distinguish the rubricator's work. *O* also has innumerable corrections and glosses (English and Latin) added by later readers.[9] One scribe wrote most of the text of *H*, with two contemporaries supplying a few brief passages on fols. 16, 17, and 20. The first auxiliary scribe (Ker's hand 2) wrote *of-forestihtode* (Hecht 55.12-14) and *Gaudentius-Bonefatius* (56.21-57.12); the second (Ker's hand 3), *he-lande* (55.31-56.9), *his-lytlum* (57.31-58.14), and *7 hæfde-licode* (64.9-17).[10] Daggers mark the entries of the thesaurus that fall within any of these five passages.

Except for some missing leaves, *C* and *H* survive undamaged, in excellent condition. The several modern transcripts, some made as early as the seventeenth century, never help establish the texts of the manuscripts.[11] *O*, however, suffered in the 1731 fire in the Cotton library; every page has lost a few words, usually around the edges. Apparently even within the past eighty years the manuscript has deteriorated further, for two late-nineteenth-century transcripts occasionally preserve letters no longer visible: Henry Johnson's unpublished transcript of 1882, and Hecht's edition, based ultimately on a transcript made by T. Oswald Cockayne in 1863.[12]

8 See Ker, *Catalogue*, MS. 60. Hecht thought that later hands made some minor corrections in *C*. For the twelfth-century Latin glosses, on fol. 20, see the above description of Clare College, Cambridge, MS. 30 (*Cl*).

9 For *O*, see Ker, *Catalogue*, MS. 182.

10 See Ker, *Catalogue*, MS. 328.

11 William Dugdale's autograph dictionary of 1644 excerpts many words from *H* (see *English Language Notes* 14 [1976] 110-12), and Junius transcribed several lengthy extracts at about the same time or a little later (Bodleian, MSS. Junius 46 and 52). In fact, according to Ker, 'the chapter-numbers in the margins [of *H*] are in the hand of Francis Junius' (*Catalogue*, MS. 328). Wanley printed Alfred's letter and a few lines from the openings of the first two books of the translation from *H* (p. 71).

12 Johnson transcribed *O* in November and December 1882 and then, in January 1883, collated the text of *C*, recording all variants for the first two books of the translation and adding a copy of fols. 147-8 of Book IV, after *O* breaks off. The transcript survives among the Chase-Johnson Papers in the Bowdoin College Library, Brunswick, Maine (see *Neuphilologische Mitteilungen* 79 [1978] 21-2). Cockayne transcribed the first 24 folios of *C* in September 1863 and subsequently added the rest of the text of *O*. He wrote all of *O*'s variants into the first part of the transcript, thereby completing the record of *O*, and some of *C*'s variants into the beginning of the rest of the transcript (see Hecht, p. II). Cockayne's materials passed to Walter Skeat and thence to Heinrich Krebs, who by 1878 had prepared his own transcript of *H* for an aborted edition of Books I and II of the translation (Hecht, p. II). Page proofs of two-thirds of the text, based on *H* with lacunae filled in from *O*, and a manuscript introduction and notes survive as Taylorian Institute, Oxford, MS. 8° E.15. Although dissuaded by Skeat from publishing his edition, Krebs printed some passages from all three manuscripts in *Anglia* (1879 and 1880). Julius Zupitza obtained the transcripts of Cockayne and Krebs and checked them, at least in part, against the manuscripts in 1882 and 1890, and Hecht checked them again in 1898 (Hecht, pp. III-IV; see also Förster's review).

The readings from *O* given in the thesaurus come directly from the manuscript; they include only undamaged or unmistakable letter forms, and square brackets set off lost or illegible parts of the text. Notes to the thesaurus, however, record any additional letters, no longer visible, seen by Hecht or Johnson.

The Old English entries have three basic formats:

ongyteþ / oncnæwð
geswenced *C*, geswencedu *O* / gedreht
nanra (nan[ ] *O*) þinga / na

The slash (/) separates the reading of Wærferth's original translation, on the left, from the reading of the revision. *Ongyteþ* without any siglum means that the form, ignoring differences of *þ*/*ð*, appears in both *C* and *O*. *H*, the unique witness of the revision, has *oncnæwð*. *C* and *O* differ in the last two examples. In the third, *C* reads *nanra þinga; O, nan[ ]þinga,* with the possible (in this instance, probable) loss of one or more letters after the second *n*. Unless stated otherwise in notes or in the word index, all the Old English readings take their word division from Hecht.

Any corresponding Latin accompanies the Old English material: first the reading of Moricca's text (with page and line number), then any variants from the collated Latin sources that may support or help explain either Old English reading. The collated sources succeed in a fixed order:

– Manuscripts collated by Moricca (as corrected by De Vogüé), in alphabetical order of sigla: *A, C, M* (begins at 23.10), O_1 (begins at 118.21), O_2, *S*, V_1, V_2, V_3, and V_4
– Manuscripts collated independently, in alphabetical order: *Bo, Cl, Hf, La,* Pa_1 (missing 16.5-16.25 and 24.7-25.13), Pa_2, *Ro* (begins at 99.10), *Sa* (begins at 42.7, missing 53.1-54.23), St_1, *Ta*, W_1 (has only 81.21-83.17, 93.17-96.20, and 131.8-133.8), and W_2 (missing 87.3-90.16)
– Manuscripts collated by Waitz for his selections (namely, 20.8-22.7, 38.8-39.5, 63.10-14, 101.3-103.15, 106.21-108.10, 109.3-5, and 122.5-9), in alphabetical order: Be_1 (missing all the passages except 101.3-103.15), Be_2 (missing 20.8-22.7), *Mu* (missing all except 106.21-108.10 and 122.5-9), St_2 (missing all except 101.3-103.15 and 122.5-9), and St_3
– The Maurists' printed edition

Two typical Latin entries illustrate the citation format:

instrueret; introduceret V_1, duceret *Maurists, var.*
inaniscerit *M;* intumesceret *Cl*

The reading of Moricca's text appears to the left of the semicolon: *instrueret* without a siglum means that the word comes from manuscript *A*, the usual source of the text. In the second example, however, Moricca used *M's inaniscerit* for the text and cited *A's* reading, *inanesceret,* in the critical apparatus. After the semicolon follow any variants that may help explain the Old English. Citing *Cl* for *intumesceret* means that none of the manuscripts which precede *Cl* on the list given above has the reading (i.e., the manuscripts used by Moricca, plus *Bo*); they either lack the passage entirely or have another reading. The sources after *Cl* on the list (*Hf, La,* etc.; the manuscripts used by Waitz; and the Maurists' edition) may or may not have *intumesceret.* Similarly, V_1 is the first manuscript on the list to read *introduceret;* the Maurists' edition is the first (and only) source that has *duceret,* as a textual variant given in their critical apparatus. All the Latin readings silently expand abbreviations, ignore manuscript capitalization, render *æ* or *ę* as *ae,* and normalize *u* and *v*. Moricca's edition provides the word division. Aside from a few instances in which it may throw light on the Old English to do so, erasures and the different hands of the manuscripts are not indicated.

One central question remains. What principles guide the selection of entries? Sometimes the reviser changed only a single word of a sentence or clause in Wærferth's original translation; just as often, though, he compressed or expanded, changed word order and syntax, or otherwise rewrote (see Hecht, *Einleitung,* pp. 29-34 and 130-34, and Potter, pp. 37-9). In passages of the former type, the corresponding words of the two versions have the same immediate context; in passages of the latter type, which words correspond? The thesaurus probably errs on the side of inclusion. But readers who question the presence of some entries also may wish to add pairs of words or phrases. In either event, readers must look up the contexts for themselves; to discuss or quote even a fraction of the passages would hopelessly increase the size of this book. For the same reason examples such as the following cannot go into the thesaurus: *gegearwode 7 gecyðde / gegearwode, bisc(e)ophad / bisceopfolgoð 7 had* (65.32, with, presumably, *H*'s reading short for **bisceopfolgoð 7 bisceophad*), and *þa / þa þing* (as well as *þæt / þa þing* [60.1]). The single word of one version turns up in the corresponding phrase of the other (see Hecht, *Einleitung,* p. 134, and Potter, p. 39).

The Old English dictionary by Clark Hall and Meritt (Clark Hall-Meritt) arbitrates most questions of word identity. The thesaurus includes *genyded / geneadode* because Clark Hall-Meritt distinguishes the Class 2 weak verb *geneadian* from its Class 1 analogue *genydan* (see under *niedan*), excludes (genitive or dative singular) *lufan / lufe* because the dictionary has only one entry, *lufu,* for 'love.'[13] On occasion, however, Clark Hall-Meritt makes two words out of what may represent only phonological variants, e.g. *ætywednes* versus *ætywnes* (the variation occurs at 19.3; see A. Campbell, §477, and Sievers-Brunner, §§197-8). As for word division, the thesaurus usually abides by Clark Hall-Meritt's decision; the only exception, certain verbs and their possible prefixes (see A. Campbell, *Addenda,* p. v). Thus *in / into* (and *in / innto* [29.2]), *nalæs / na,* and *þætte / þæt* appear in the thesaurus; *in / in on* (30.31, 57.12, 58.10, 125.25, 152.21), *sylf / him sylf,* and *swa / swa swa* or *þa / þa þa* do not. Despite Hecht's word division, supported by Clark Hall-Meritt, *steah* C, *stag* O / *instah* (24.2) and many other examples like it do not qualify, because *instah* has the same meaning as **stah in* (Clark Hall-Meritt defines *instigan* as 'to climb in' [p. 206]; see also A. Campbell, §§78-81). But *cidde / ofercidde* (132.24) goes in the thesaurus since *ofercidan* means 'to chide sharply' (Clark Hall-Meritt, p. 255), not 'to chide over.' And *wunað / þurhwunað* (86.10), though lying somewhere in between, also goes in. Similarly, Hecht's *æfterfarende / æfterfyliende* and *oferstah / innstah* appear in the thesaurus as *farende / fyliende* and *ofer / inn,* respectively, but *þurheode* C, *þurhleornode* O / *þurhferde* (136.4) appears without change (cf. *þurhleoriað ne ... ongytað* C, *þurhleorniað ne ... ongitað* O / *þurhfarað* [138.29]). The notes give Hecht's word division whenever it differs from that of the thesaurus. Aside from a few well-chosen exceptions, the thesaurus includes only those words or phrases that belong to the same part of speech or perform the same function in the clause.

Often *O* has suffered damage in places where *C* and *H* disagree, e.g.:

60.26 folgian *C,* fyl[ ]n *O* / fylian
66.21 comon *C,* [ ]comon *O* / becomon
14.24 becom *C,* [ ]cwom *O* / [ ]com
68.26 *om. C,* g[ ]g[ ] *O* / begiten

At 60.26, *O* when intact almost certainly had the word found in *H.* At 66.21, however, *O* may

13 The reviser often declined *lufu* strong when Wærferth had declined it weak (3.29, 8.14, 8.21, 17.12, 17.19, 33.33, 47.2, 62.26, 96.27, 101.6, 110.7 [11x]). Other nouns that may belong to different declensions include *bryce* (82.27), *burn* (94.14), *flan* (114.34), *gecynd* (44.22), *geþyld* (20.16), *hæte* (162.31), *hlæder* (45.29), *landleod* (97.31), *mægen* (71.5), *mann* (75.10, 144.6), *maniend* (157.32), *netel* (101.17), *oferhygd* (144.27), *onsittend* (15.10), *þeow* (37.23, 38.24, 133.18, 157.30), and *weorðmynd* (103.20). Somewhat inconsistently, Clark Hall-Meritt does in fact provide two entries for a few of these nouns.

once have agreed with *C*. The thesaurus excludes the first example and the others similar to it (136.13 [*C* omits the passage] and 138.12) but includes the second and its like (95.28, 128.9, 134.16, 144.23, and 162.27). The last two examples both appear in the thesaurus. At 14.24, *C* and *H* may once have agreed: *H*'s preceding leaf, now lost, may have ended with *be*, giving *becom* for the revision. At 68.26, *C* uses a construction not comparable with that of the other manuscripts; but regardless of what letters *O* wants, it certainly disagreed with *H* (cf. 136.14 om. C, *ge[ ]nesse* O / *godcundnysse*).

Because of evidence that inflectional vowels have fallen together in all three manuscripts of the translation, the thesaurus does not include differences such as *onstyred* / *onstyrod* (74.3).[14] Since, according to A. Campbell, 'in OE [the passive participle] usually has the prefix *ge-* if the verb has not some other unaccented prefix' (§731(h)), differences between verbs with and without the prefix also do not appear whenever the form with *ge* is a past (or 'passive') participle and the form without it is not (25.6, 28.9, 31.7, 34.6 [om. *O*], 86.6, 86.7, 115.23, 136.23, 143.14, and 171.27). Names do not belong in a thesaurus, but the different forms given to Rome, or Roman, and Jewish deserve mention:

30.25 Romebyrig / Romanabyri[15]
31.3 Romana orbe (*M*)

52.3 Romane / Romaniscean
47.13 Romanae

132.31 Romesbyrig *C*, Romebyrig *O* / Rome
102.10 Romam

133.8 Romesbyrig *C*, Romebyrig *O* / Rome
102.13 Romam

133.22 Romeburge / Romanaburge
103.3 Romanae orbis

107.26 Iudea / Iudeisces
82.16 Iudaeorum *M*

The two versions of the translation also differ several times over less common names (40.28, 41.27, 83.27, 96.9, 102.9, 131.8 [2x]). Also cf. 34.24 *Romana biscope (bisceope* O*)* / *Romanebyri* (33.11 *Romanae orbis*).

Two of the revisions of Wærferth's original translation – *gyta (gita)* for *gyt (git, giet)* and *on* for *in* – are very numerous and unlikely to have been chosen on the basis of the Latin text; to save space, they are presented below as a unit rather than individually in the thesaurus:

gyt, git, *or* giet / gyta *or* gita 20.7, 32.33, 33.18, 36.16 (*om. C*), 37.15 (*O has* git, *not* giet *as reported by Hecht*), 42.19, 51.28, 56.22 *(one of the auxiliary scribes wrote this passage in H*), 57.16, 61.22, 62.21, 79.24, 83.10, 83.23, 86.2, 86.13, 95.4, 96.15, 102.27, 128.34, 128.35, 138.20, 138.28, 139.32, 145.28, 147.6, 151.28, 170.8 [28x]

14 Many examples of vowel confusion occur in *C* and *H* (e.g. 45.2 *slitað* C, 101.15 *þære* H), few in *O* (e.g. 60.28 *unforspornenen*, 145.33 *geunrotseden*). Variations between the abstract suffixes *ing* and *ung* appear in the thesaurus, however (see A. Campbell, §383, and Sievers-Brunner, §142, A.). Following Bosworth-Toller, the thesaurus admits *middaneard* and *middangeard* as two words (see 53.28, 173.32, and 174.1) but takes *wineard* and *wingeard* (at 88.17) as variants of the same word (see also Campbell, §303, n., and Sievers-Brunner, §214.7).

15 Hecht printed *Romana byri* for his text of *H*, then closed up the form in his 'Berichtigungen' at the end of the edition (after p. 374).

in / on 3.7, 4.21, 5.21, 6.27, 6.29, 7.7, 7.35, 8.4, 8.8, 9.11, 9.12, 15.20, 15.33, 16.6, 16.7, 16.21, 18.3, 19.3, 22.25, 22.29, 22.34, 23.21 (*om. O*), 24.8, 24.24, 25.8, 25.26, 26.4, 26.15, 27.7, 27.16, 27.17, 28.22 [2x], 29.30, 30.1, 30.24, 31.11, 31.32, 32.28, 34.14, 35.13, 38.30, 39.25, 39.33, 40.27, 40.33, 41.3, 41.6, 41.17, 41.29, 42.25, 43.23, 43.24, 43.32 (*def. O*), 44.9, 44.17, 45.4, 45.28, 51.2, 51.15 (*Hecht printed* in gegotene (geoten *O*) *for CO and* ongoten *for H*), 51.33, 53.21, 53.28, 53.32, 55.5, 56.17, 57.15, 57.27, 58.12 (*one of the auxiliary scribes wrote this passage in H*), 58.33, 59.14 (*om. C*), 60.24 (*for O's text, Hecht made out only* n; *read* in), 61.1, 63.12 (*Hecht printed* ineardiend *and* oneardiend), 63.16, 63.27, 64.30, 65.14, 65.16 (*def. O*), 65.22, 66.15, 67.28, 67.29, 69.4, 69.26, 69.30, 70.13, 70.26, 72.23 (*CO has* gangende (goncgende *O*) in *beside H's* ingangende on), 73.1, 73.24, 73.28, 74.20, 74.24 (*om. C*), 75.14, 75.23, 75.24, 75.34, 77.3, 77.33, 78.12, 81.22, 83.25, 86.25, 87.1, 87.19, 87.33, 88.3, 88.22, 88.29, 95.18, 95.24, 96.7, 96.16, 96.28, 97.28, 97.30 (*O has* hi, *not* in *as reported by Hecht*), 97.33, 101.3, 101.5, 101.25, 102.21, 102.28, 104.3, 106.29, 107.4, 108.4, 108.14, 108.17, 108.21, 109.16, 110.8, 114.13, 114.15, 114.24, 114.29 (*def. O*), 115.7, 116.6, 117.27 (*Hecht printed* inæled *and* onæled), 118.9, 118.22, 123.19 (*def. O*), 123.28, 124.5, 124.6, 124.25, 124.34 (*def. O*), 126.23 (*om. C*), 127.25, 130.9, 130.18, 131.22, 134.3, 134.6, 134.32, 135.26 (*om. C*), 137.14, 137.32, 139.8, 139.28, 141.3, 141.11, 142.7, 142.20, 142.25, 143.11, 143.24, 144.4, 144.25 (*Hecht reported O as defective; read* i[ ]), 144.33, 145.4, 145.8, 145.26, 145.34, 146.7 (*Hecht printed* inlihteð *and* onlihteð), 146.34, 147.34, 148.17, 150.6 (*def. O*), 150.9, 150.28, 151.4, 152.22, 158.8, 158.10, 158.22, 162.12, 169.6, 169.8, 169.18, 169.21, 169.23, 169.26, 169.30, 170.17, 170.19, 170.21, 170.26, 171.8, 171.17, 171.20, 172.4, 173.7, 173.10, 173.14, 173.16, 173.28, 173.33, 174.10, 174.12 [210x]

Compare 28.14 *on / into* and 141.15 *in* (def. O) *him / þæron,* both included in the thesaurus. For the distribution of the prepositions *in* and *on* in the three manuscripts, see Potter, p. 39, and *Manuscripta* 21 (1977) 38-41.

ACKNOWLEDGEMENTS

Dr. Bruce Mitchell, of St. Edmund Hall, Oxford, inadvertently originated this book when he introduced me to the *Dialogues* in 1973. A grant from the Department of English at Columbia University helped the work along, as did advice and encouragement from Dr. Malcolm Godden of Exeter College, Oxford, Professor Roberta Frank of the University of Toronto, and Professor Fred Robinson of Yale. Publication was assisted by a grant to the University of Toronto Press from the Andrew W. Mellon Foundation.

D.Y.
October 1978

the thesaurus

the thesaurus

1* 1.3 gearolice ***C, om. O*** / cuðlice
2* 1.4 gesægene ***C, om. O*** / rædinge
3* 1.5 þætte ***C, om. O*** / þæt
4* 1.6 heanesse ***C, om. O*** / healicnysse
5* 1.9 betwix ***C, om. O*** / betweoh
6* 1.10 ymbhigdo ***C, om. O*** / carfulnysse
7* 1.18 gescyrped ***C, om. O*** / getrymmed
8 2.22 forþon / cuðlice
9 3.5 ær ***C, def. O*** / for
10 3.8 genyded / geneadode
13.3 **cogimur**
11 3.9 gewiss ***C,*** gewis ***O*** / cuð
13.4 **certum**
12 3.28 gebunden / geþeoded
14.1 **obstrictus; adstrictus *S***
13 4.1 ac / leof
14.3 **numquidnam; numquid *Pa*$_1$**
14 4.2 aht / ænig þing
14.3 **aliquid**
15 4.4 gewuna / gewunelic
14.3 **solito**
16 4.6 dreoge / þolie
14.5 **patior**
17 4.6 daga gehwylce / dæghwamlice
14.5 **cotidie**
18 4.9 for / þurh
14.6 **per**
19 4.10 gecnyssed (gecnys[ ] ***O***) 7 gedrefed / onstyred
14.7 **pulsatus**
20 4.11 for / mid
21 4.12 bysgunge / abysgegunge
14.6 **occupationis**
22 4.12 hwilc ***C,*** hwylc ***O*** / hu
14.7 **qualis**
23 4.18 naht ***C,*** noht ***O*** / nan þing
14.9 **nulla**
24 4.23 sceawunge / besceawunge
14.11 **contemplatione**
25 4.25 fullneah ***C,*** fulneah ***O*** / forneah
14.12 **paena**
26 4.28 gewinnes / geswinces
14.13 **laboris**
27 4.30 scire / carfulnysse
14.13 **curae**
28 4.30 þrowað / þolað
14.14 **patitur**
29 4.32 onsyne / hiwe
14.15 **speciem**
30 4.33 ræste / stilnysse
14.15 **quietis**
31 5.2 ymb ***C,*** embe ***O*** / to
14.16 **ad**
32 5.2 oðerra (oþera ***O***) manna / yttrum
14.16 **exteriora**
33 5.3 wisan / þingum
34 5.5 buton tweon / untwylice
14.17 **procul dubio**
35 5.7 medmare / læs
14.17 **minor**
36 5.8 gehycgè ***C,*** gehicge ***O*** / geþence
14.17 **perpendo**
37 5.13 ræfnige / þolige
14.19 **porto**
38 5.13 geseoh / geþenc
14.19 **ecce**
39 5.16 mycclan (micles ***O***) sæs / sælicum
15.1 **magni maris**
40 5.28 on sæ / ut
41 5.29 swa / þæt
42 5.30 nænig / nan
43 6.1 unmætum / ormætum
15.4 **inmensis**
44 6.3 ageþencan ***C,*** ageþencean ***O*** / onbeþencean
15.5 **videre**
45 6.14 na ***C,*** no ***O*** / furðon
15.8 **neque**
46 6.15 gemyneþ / þurh gemynd ... begymð
15.8 **per memoriam videat**
47 6.15 þe / þæt
15.9 **quod**
48 6.15 hæfde / mid dædum geheold
15.9 **per actione (occasionem *V*$_1$) tenebat**

3* *C* has the abbreviated form *ꝥte; H* has *ꝥ.* **19** Hecht reported *gecnys[ ]gedrefed* for *O.* **37** A later hand has glossed *O*'s *ræfnige* with *þolie.* See the note to entry **232.** **45** Hecht reported *forðon* for *H.* **47** *H* abbreviates *ꝥ.*

49 6.16 forþon / be þam
15.9 **unde**
50 6.20 7 (ond *O*) eac / soðlice
15.11 **vero**
51 6.20 fulloft *C*, fuloft *O* / foroft
15.11 **nonnumquam**
52 6.30 næfre / a
15.16 **ne; nec, c** ***erased Ta***
53 6.34 gewinnum / geswinceum
15.17 **laboribus**
54 7.1 nu / eallunga
15.18 **iam**
55 7.2 asceade *C*, gesceade *O* / tosceade
15.20 **distinguo**
56 7.6 naht *C*, noht *O* / na
15.21 **non; iam** ***Pa_2***
57 7.8 asceonan *C*, ascinon *O* / scinon
15.22 **fuisse; fulsisse** ***A***
58 7.11 þære *C*, ðæra *O* / hyra
15.22 **quorum**
59 7.12 naht *C*, noht *O* / nan þing
15.23 **quidem ... non**
60 7.14 þonne ... hwæþre (hwæðere *O*) / swaþeah
15.24 **tamen**
61 7.15 þætte / þæt
62 7.20 7swarode / cwæð
63 7.21 eala / la
64 7.22 asecge / arecce
15.27 **referam**
65 7.22 fullmedemum *C*, fulmedemum *O* / fulfremedum
15.27 **perfectis**
66 7.23 gecorenum / afandodum
15.27 **probatis-**
67 7.24 yfellic *C*, yfelic *O* / waclic
15.28 **homuncio**
68 7.24 ongeat / oncneow
16.1 **agnovi**
69 7.29 blinneð / geendige
16.2 **cessabit**
70 7.32 hwæthugu *C*, hwæthwega *O* / sum þing
16.3 **aliqua**
71 7.33 hefig / hefilic
16.4 **grave**
72 8.1 cymð *C*, cymeð *O* / sprungen
16.5 **oritur**
73 8.1 naht (noht *O*) ungelic ... ac ... geþwærlicu / gelic
16.5 **non dispar**
74 8.2 trymnes / trymming
16.5 **aedificatio**
75 8.5 ongytan / oncnawen
16.7 **agnoscitur**
76 8.6 byþ / sy
16.6 **sit**
77 8.7 7 / soðlice
16.7 **vero**
78 8.8 segene *C*, sægene *O* / cyðnysse
16.7 **narratione**
79 8.10 gemæred *C*, gemærsod *O* / geswutelod
16.8 **declaratur**
80 8.11 full *C*, ful *O* / forwel
16.8 **nonnulli**
81 8.12 getihtað / tihtað
16.9 **succendunt; accendunt** ***Bo***
82 8.12 bysna *C*, bysene *O* / gebysnunga
16.9 **exempla**
83 8.15 7 (ond *O*) swa / eac
16.10 **vero**
84 8.17 on *C*, in *O* / þurh
16.11 **in**
85 8.18 bysenum / gebysnunga
16.11 **exemplis**
86 8.19 onbærned / onæled
16.12 **accenditur**
87 8.20 foregangendra *C*, bysena locendra *O* / forestæppendra
16.12 **praecedentium**
88 8.25 ongyteþ / oncnæwð
16.13 **cognoverit; agnoverit** ***Hf***
89 8.27 7swarode / cwæð
90 8.27 wisan / þing
16.15 **ea**
91 8.28 æt / þurh
92 8.29 untwygendlice *C*, untweogendlice *O* / untwylice
16.16 **incunctanter**

49 The rubricator supplied *O*'s *þon*. **57** De Vogüé has reported *fulsisse* for *A* (p. 330). **61** *C* abbreviates *ꝥte; H* has *ꝥ*. **72** Hecht printed *upsprungen* for *H*, beside *CO*'s *cym(e)ð ... upp.*

93 8.29 secge *C*, [ ]secge *O* / gecyðe
16.16 **narro**
94 8.31 cuþ / cuðlice
16.17 **luce clarius**
95 8.32 writon / awriton
16.18 **discripserunt; scripserunt** V_2
96 9.1 þæt *C*, þi þe *O* / forþy þe
97 9.5 animan 7 ateon / ætbrede
16.19 **subtraham**
98 9.7 tweonge *C*, tweounge *O* / twynunge
16.19 **dubitationis**
99 9.7 æt / be
16.19 **per**
100 9.8 write / awrite
16.20 **discribo**
101 9.10 þa / hy
16.20 **haec**
102 9.15 animan / niman
16.23 **tenere**
103 9.19 gecoplice / coplice
16.24 **apte**
104 14.24 becom *C*, [ ]cwom *O* / [ ]com
21.3 **pervenit**
105 14.28 blodgian *C*, blodigean *O* / wundian
21.5 **cruentare**
106 15.4 geblodgode *C*, geblodegade *O* / mistucode
21.6 **cruentati**
107 15.4 þehhweðre *C*, hwæðere *O* / swaþeah
21.5 **tamen**
108 15.7 7 / ac
21.7 **-que**
109 15.8 efne swa swa / swilce
21.7 **quasi**
110 15.19 cyrdon / gecyrdon
21.11 **-versi**
111 15.24 gangað *C*, gongað *O* / farað
21.13 **ite**
112 15.24 mid gode / teala ... wel
21.13 **cum bono**
113 15.26 þearfe / neod
21.13 **opus**
114 15.27 mid nyde (nede *O*) / neadlunga
21.14 **invitum; invictum** V_1
115 15.29 fram *C*, from *O* / þanon
21.15 **ab-**
116 15.31 hræde / hrædlicum
21.15 **tanto**
117 15.32 oferferan / oferfaran
21.16 **transire**
118 15.33 swa swa / swilce
21.16 **ac si**
119 15.34 mænigne *C*, nænigne *O* / nænne
21.17 **minime**
120 15.35 gelamp *C*, gelomp *O* / geworden
21.17 **factum**
121 16.1 mæn *C*, menn *O* / þeowe
21.18 **servo**
122 16.3 onfengon *C*, onfe[ ]gon *O* / underfengon
21.19 **receperentur**
123 16.6 tid / timan
21.19 **tempore**
124 16.10 gaacsode *C*, geaxode *O* / gehyrde
22.1 **exierat**
125 16.12 mannes *C*, monnes *O* / þeowes
22.1 **famuli**
126 16.15 gangan *C*, geondgan *O* / steppan
22.2 **-gressi**
127 16.18 hwær / þærþær
22.3 **ubi**
128 16.22 gelamp *C*, gelomp *O* / geworden
22.4 *om.;* **est** *erased Bo*
129 16.23 wise / þing
22.4 **res**
130 16.23 þa *C*, þon ða *O* / þonne
131 16.25 on / æt
22.5 **in**
132 16.27 þehhwæðre *C*, hwæðre *O* / swaþeah
133 17.2 tid / timan
22.8 **tempore**
134 17.5 underfeng (underfencg *O*) 7 ... heold / wæs ... hyrde
22.9 **successerat**
135 17.19 for / mid
136 17.21 mannes *C*, namnes *O* / weres

96 *C* abbreviates *ꝥ*. **130** Hecht did not report *O*'s adverb or conjunction *ða*.

137	17.21	bridelse / bridele
	22.14	**frenum**
138	17.23	nænigra (nænige *O*) þinga / natoþæshwon
	22.15	**nullatenus**
139	17.24	fram *C*, freo *O* / heonon
	22.15	**re-**
140	17.24	ær ðon (ðan *O*) / buton
	22.15	**nisi**
141	17.27	þyllic *C*, þis ðyslice *O* / swilc
	22.16	**tale**
142	17.30	ðære / hire
	22.16	**illius**
143	17.30	geornfullan *C*, geornfullan ... halsunge *O* / halsiendlican
	22.17	**iuramentum**
144	17.32	nænigra *C*, nænige *O* / nan
	22.17	**nequaquam**
145	17.32	ac / þa ... la
146	17.32	fealh / smeade
	22.18	**haesit**
147	18.2	sceawian 7 smeagean / asmeagean
	22.18	**considerare**
148	18.2	hulic / hwilc
	22.18	**quale**
149	18.3	camp / gecamp
	22.19	**certamen**
150	18.5	feaht / wann ... fleat
	22.19	**pugnabat**
151	18.8	unlifigendan / deadan
152	18.10	nyþde *C*, neðde *O* / gedyrstlæhte
	22.20	**praesumeret**
153	18.12	wilnode *C*, [ ]willade *O* / gewilnode
154	18.12	swa / eac to þam
155	18.13	mildheort / earmheort
156	18.13	þuhte sarlic / ofhreow
	22.21	**dolor**
157	18.14	earman / sarlican dreorinysse
	22.21	**orbatae**
158	18.19	nanra þinga *C*, nane þincga *O* / na
	22.23	**enim**
159	18.20	hreowsung *C*, hreowsuncg *O* / behreowsung
	22.23	**pietas**
160	18.21	arwyrðan / mildheortnysse
161	18.22	oferswyðde *C*, oferswiþde *O* / geliðegode
	22.24	**vicisset**
162	18.31	cwicne / libbendne
	23.1	**viventem**
163	18.33	ongan / begann
	23.2	**coeperat**
164	18.34	frægn *C*, fræg[ ] *O* / cwæð
165	19.1	geearnung *C*, geæarnuncg *O* / earnung
	23.4	**meritum**
166	19.3	7swarode *C*, ondswerede *O* / andwyrde
167	19.4	foretacnes / tacnes
	23.5	**signi**
168	19.7	forðon / eac
	23.6	**adque; enim** *C*
169	19.10	ma / swyðor
	23.7	**plus**
170	19.11	þæs / his
	23.8	**cuius**
171	19.13	tweon / twynunge
	23.9	**-mirum**
172	19.15	swa / soðlice
	23.10	**nam**
173	19.15	sægd / awriten
	23.10	**aestimavit; existimavit** V_3
174	19.17	come / becom
	23.11	**veniens**
175	19.18	sciccels *C*, siccels *O* / reaf
	23.10	**pallium**
176	19.22	nanra (nan[ ] *O*) þinga / na
	23.12	**menime** *M*
177	19.23	7 (ond *O*) ... swa / þa
	23.12	**sed cum**
178	19.26	sciccelse / reafe
	23.13	**pallio**
179	19.33	gegearwian *C*, gegearwigean *O* / begitan

159 Hecht reported *hreowsung* for *O*. **165** Hecht reported *geearnuncg* for *O*. **175** *O*'s rubricator supplied a phrase containing *siccels*. **176** In *O*, part of a letter remains visible after the second *n;* probably part of an *e*, given the several examples of *nanra* C, *nane* O (18.19, 60.19, 158.2, 164.14 (*na[ ]* O), 167.17, and 243.25; but cf. 219.16 *nanra* C, *nænige* O). Hecht reported *næni[ ]ðinga* for *O*.

23.15 **exhibere**
180 19.34 gelædde *C*, lædde *O* / geteah
23.16 **reduxit; duxit** *M*
181 20.3 worhte / geworhte
23.18 **fecit**
182 20.5 lysteþ / licað
23.19 **libet**
183 20.7 frigne / bidde
23.19 **quaeso**
184 20.7 aht / ænig þing
23.19 **aliquid**
185 20.7 oþres / mare
23.20 **aliut** *M*
186 20.9 getrymnysse *C*, try[ ]nysse *O* / trymminge
23.20 **aedificationem**
187 20.12 ⁊swarode *C*, ondswerode *O* / cwæð to
188 20.12 witodlice / gewislice
23.22 **plane**
189 20.14 hwær / hwæðer
23.22 **si**
190 20.14 se / ænig
191 20.14 onhyrgean / geefenlæcean
23.22 **imitari**
192 20.17 foretacnu / tacna
23.23 **signis**
193 20.19 se / þe
23.24 **qui**
194 20.24 æfæstan *C*, erfæstan *O* / arwurðan
23.25 **venerabilem**
195 20.26 forbeah / hetelice beot
24.1 **excederit; cederet** V_3, **caederet** *Maurists*
196 20.27 gyrde / repel
24.2 **virgam**
197 20.27 sleanne *C*, sleande *O* / þersceanne
24.2 **ferire**
198 20.28 gefeng *C*, gefencg *O* / gelæhte
24.2 **conpraehenso**
199 20.28 æt ... foran / ætforan
200 20.29 ręste *C*, reste *O* / bedde
201 20.32 asweoll *C*, asweol *O* / toswollen
24.4 **tumentem**
202 20.33 geswungen / mid geþersce mistucod
24.5 **caesus**
203 20.34 ræste *C*, reste *O* / bedde
24.5 **stratum**
204 21.1 ane / sume
205 21.2 ymb / for
24.6 **pro**
206 21.2 neodþearfe *C*, neadþearfe *O* / þearfe
24.6 **utilitate**
207 21.6 ræste *C*, reste *O* / bedde
24.7 **lectum**
208 21.9 man *C*, monn *O* / wer
209 21.10 gearod *C*, gearad *O* / gearwurðod
24.9 **honoraretur; veneraretur** *Bo*
210 21.16 gangan / faran
24.11 **ire**
211 21.17 min / leof
212 21.22 ⁊ *C*, ond *O* / hwæt
213 21.23 in / of
24.14 **a; pro** *Bo*
214 21.23 ingehigdum *C*, ingehygdum *O* / inneweardre
24.14 **fundo**
215 21.24 sceawode *C*, sceawade *O* / besceawode
24.14 **considerans**
216 21.24 sylfes *C*, seolfes *O* / agene
24.14 **suam**
217 21.25 gelice / ⁊
218 21.27 manþwærnysse *C*, monðwærnesse *O* / geþwærnysse
24.15 **mansuitudinem**
219 21.28 hraþe astylde *C*, hwæde[ ] *O* / forð aræsde
24.15 **prosilivit** *C*
220 21.28 ræste *C*, reste *O* / bedde
24.15 **lecto** *C*
221 21.30 cyðde / cwæð
24.16 **testatus**
222 21.33 geearnunge / mærum
24.17 **tali-**

194 Hecht reported *irfæstan* for *O*. **210** The rubricator supplied the first *n* in *O*. **219** Hecht reported *hræðe[ ]* for *O*.

223 21.33 man *C*, mon *O* / were
24.17 **viro**
224 21.33 swylce / swa
24.17 **tam**
225 21.33 wælhreownysse *C*, wælreow-
nesse *O* / wælhreowne
24.17 **crudelem**
226 21.34 fraceþa *C*, fraced *O* / teonan
24.17 **contumeliam**
227 21.34 gefremede / gedyde
24.17 **facere**
228 21.34 ongæn þan *C*, ondgegn ðon *O* /
þærongean
24.18 **contra**
229 22.2 sæde *C*, sægde *O* / cwæð
24.19 **referebat**
230 22.3 sylfes / agenum
24.19 **suae**
231 22.4 uncysta / reðnysse
24.19 **saevitiae**
232 22.6 aræfnode *C*, aræfnde *O* /
þolode
24.20 **pertulerat**
233 22.7 gedon / geworden
24.20 **actum; factum** ***Bo***
234 22.7 fæder / abbod
24.21 **pater**
235 22.8 modþwærnysse *C*, monþwær-
nesse *O* / geþwærnysse
24.20 **mansuitudinem**
236 22.8 gelæded / getogen
24.21 **perduceretur**
237 22.9 geweard / wearð
24.22 **fierit** ***M***
238 22.13 farende / ferde
24.23 **-gressus**
239 22.14 manige *C*, monige *O* / fela
24.23 **multi**
240 22.15 æþelcunde / æðelborene
24.23 **nobiles**
241 22.17 arodon *C*, aredon *O* /
arwurðedon
24.24 **honorabant**
242 22.17 þa eac / 7
243 22.24 geslægen *C*, geslegen *O* / getucod
25.4 **pertuli**
244 22.26 are / wurðmynd
25.4 **honorem** ***C***
245 22.27 fæder 7 ... lareowes / abbodes
25.5 **magistri nec patris**
246 22.28 uncysta / unþeawa
25.5 **vitium**
247 22.28 geypte / ameldode
25.5 **prodebat**
248 22.30 georn / bearn
25.6 **-currebat**
249 22.34 sægdest / rehtest
25.8 **retulisti**
250 23.1 þeowa (ðeawa *O*) 7 ... clænan
lifes / mægena
25.9 **virtutibus**
251 23.2 onhergend *C*, onhyrgend *O* /
efenlæcendras
25.9 **imitatores**
252 23.8 ær / eac
253 23.9 ful (genog *O*) geare / wel
25.11 **bene**
254 23.14 hwelchugu *C*, hwylchuge *O* /
sume
25.13 **aliqua**
255 23.14 word / þing
256 23.15 coman *C*, comon *O* / becumað
25.13 **veniunt; redeunt** Pa_1
257 23.17 7 / ac
25.14 **sed**
258 23.22 godes ... 7 mycelre (micelre *O*)
geearnunge / mæres
25.16 **magnae**
259 23.26 geard / hege
25.17 **saepem**
260 23.33 genumene / fornumene
25.19 **direpta**
261 23.35 þa ætnexstan (ætnehstan *O*) /
oðþæt
262 24.2 geard / hege
263 24.4 funde / gemette
26.1 **repperit**
264 24.8 ofer / inn
265 24.12 behealde / gehealde
26.4 **custodias**

232 A later hand has glossed *O*'s *aræfnde* with *þolede*. See the note to entry **37**. 238 Hecht printed *utfarende* and *utferde*. 264 Hecht printed *oferstah* and *innstah*.

266 24.15 hraðe *C*, raðe *O* / þa hræddlice
26.5 **protinus; protinus ergo** *Cl*

267 24.17 gestildon 7 gereston / stille wæron
26.7 **quiescerent**

268 24.19 gewunelic þeaw *C*, gewunlic *O* / gewuna
26.7 **more solito**

269 24.20 geard / hege
26.7 **saepem**

270 24.21 ofdune / nyðer
26.8 *om;* **de-** *C*

271 24.24 afyrhted / afæred
26.9 **tremefactus; tremens factus** *M*

272 24.25 afeoll / hreas
26.9 **-cidit**

273 24.25 ofduneweard *C*, ofdunweard *O* / nyðerweard
26.9 **con-; ce-** Pa_1

274 24.27 sagle (sahle *O*) ... geardes / hegesahle
26.10 **sude (acuti** *as a gloss La*, **palo** Pa_2**) saepis**

275 24.28 adune *C*, ofdune *O* / nyþer
26.11 **deorsum**

276 25.1 þider þe *C*, to ðæs þe *O* / swa hwider swa

277 25.2 þa / 7

278 25.2 hraðe / sona
26.14 **ilico; statim** *Maurists*

279 25.5 þis *C*, ðus *or* ðiis *O* / nu

280 25.6 forhwon / hu
26.15 **quare**

281 25.6 gedyrstigodest *C*, gedyrstgadest *O* / gedyrstlæhtest
26.16 **praesumpsisti**

282 25.8 wyrtune / geswince
26.15 **labore**

283 25.9 æfter / mid

284 25.10 onlysde / ahlinode
26.17 **solvit**

285 25.10 gærde *C*, gearde *O* / hege
26.17 **sepe**

286 25.12 ofdune / nyðer
26.18 **de-**

287 25.14 wyrtgeardes / wyrttunes
26.19 **horti**

288 25.15 gehwylce *C*, gehwelce *O* / þa

289 25.17 wynsumnysse / werednysse
26.20 **dulcidine; dulcitudinem** *M*

290 25.19 stala / stel
26.21 **furtum ... facias**

291 25.19 na (ne *O*) ma / nan þing
26.21 **non**

292 25.20 sy *C*, si *O* / beo
26.21 **habes**

293 25.20 ga / gang
26.22 **-gredere**

294 25.21 her / hider
26.21 **hinc; huc** *C*, **hic** V_2

295 25.22 begeate *C*, begete *O* / gename
26.22 **tollere**

296 25.23 estfulnesse *C*, estfullnesse *O* / estfullum mode
26.23 **devotus**

297 25.24 swa *C*, swa swa *O* / þæs þe
27.1 **ut**

298 25.25 holenga / on idel
27.1 **incassum**

299 25.25 nænige / nane
27.1 **non**

300 25.27 mægnu 7 tacnu *C*, mægenu 7 tacenu *O* / wundortacnu
27.2 **signa**

301 25.31 7swarode *C*, andswarode *O* / cwæð

302 26.4 man *C*, monn *O* / wer
27.6 **vir**

303 26.10 geearnunge / halinysse
27.7 **admirationis**

304 26.12 butan tweon / soðlice
28.2 **nimirum**

305 26.13 haligdomes / halinysse
28.2 **sanctitatis**

306 26.14 hlaford / lareow
28.3 **pater**

307 26.15 þa / witodlice
28.4 **cum**

308 26.15 tid / timan
28.4 **tempore**

273 Pa_1 has *cecidit*, possibly for **secidit*. 279 *O*'s two minims may represent either a *u* or *ii;* cf. *tiid(e)* (27.14, 34.29, 51.33), *-cliif* (52.16), and many other examples of *ii* in *O*. Hecht printed *ðus*.

309 26.16 grimmum *C*, grimme *O* / teartum
28.4 **agri; grandi V_4**

310 26.18 nearonessa *C*, nearognesse *O* / angsumnyssa
28.5 **angustiae**

311 26.20 teolunge *C*, gimene *O* / bigenge
28.5 **studium**

312 26.20 godcundra beboda / gebeda
28.5 **orationis**

313 26.22 wisan / þinge
28.6 **re**

314 26.25 se / he

315 26.26 ealle *C*, eall *O* / ælce
28.8 **omnem**

316 26.27 cennendan leomu *C*, gecynd-limu *O* / cennendlicum limum
28.9 **genitalibus membris**

317 26.29 efne (emne *O*) swa / swilce
28.10 **ac si**

318 26.30 had / wæpnedhad
28.10 **sexum**

319 26.31 wæs / wearð

320 26.31 gebælded *C*, gehealden *O* / gestrangod
28.11 **fretus**

321 26.32 of / þurh
28.11 **ex**

322 27.1 wera ealdorman (ealdormonn *O*) / ealdor wæpnedmanna
28.12 **viris ... prae-**

323 27.4 blan *C*, blonn *O* / geswac
28.13 **cessabat**

324 27.4 hwæðre / swaþeah
28.13 **tamen**

325 27.5 næfre / ne
28.14 **ne; nec St_1**

326 27.6 gelyfdon *C*, gelifdon *O* / getruwodon
28.14 **crederent**

327 27.7 wisan / þingum
28.14 **re**

328 27.14 tide *C*, tiide *O* / timan
28.16 **tempore**

329 27.15 scincræftigan *C*, scincræftgan *O* / drycræfton
28.16 **malifici**

330 27.18 munuchade / munucreafe
29.1 **monachico *C* (monastico *A*, monachi V_1) habitu**

331 27.23 gehihte / hopode
29.3 **postolavit; speravit *C*, petivit V_3, impetravit *La***

332 27.33 in / into
29.6 **in**

333 28.2 min / leof

334 28.5 sylf / swutol

335 28.8 tyðian *C*, tiðian *O* / getiðian
29.9 **praestare**

336 28.10 wer / þeow
29.10 **famulus**

337 28.14 on / into
29.13 **in**

338 28.16 naht manegum *C*, monegum *O* / feawum
29.13 **non ... multos**

339 28.17 man *C*, mon *O* / þeow
29.14 **famulus**

340 28.18 trymmanne *C*, trymmenne *O* / lærenne
29.14 **exortandis**

341 28.20 wyllan *C*, willan *O* / gewilnungum
29.14 **desideria**

342 28.26 wæs / wearð

343 28.28 brogan *C*, *om.* *O* / hreame
30.4 **stridoribus**

344 28.29 gristbitingum *C*, gri[ ] *O* / gristbitunge
30.4 **[stridoribus]**

345 28.33 þurh / mid
30.5 **per**

346 29.1 hlafordes / ealdres
30.6 **patris**

347 29.2 æfweardnysse *C*, æfweardnesse *O* / framsiþe
30.6 **absentia *C***

348 29.2 gan / gangan
30.6 **accedere**

349 29.2 in / innto

350 29.7 7 *C*, ond *O* / ac

344 Hecht reported *O* as defective. Both *brogan* and *gristbitingum*, or *hreame* and *gristbitunge*, render *stridoribus.*

	30.9	*om.;* ergo *Hf*, -que W_2
351	29.7	sona / hrædlice
	30.9	**repente**
352	29.7	sændon *C*, sendon *O* / asend
	30.9	**missum**
353	29.9	bodedon *C*, bodedan *O* / gecydde
	30.10	**nuntiatum**
354	29.10	inhæted / getyrfed
	30.11	**aestuaret**
355	29.10	unmætum / ormætum
	30.10	**inmensis**
356	29.14	man / wer
	30.12	**vir**
357	29.14	hloh *C*, ahloh *O* / smercode
	30.12	**subrisit**
358	29.16	hwæt *C*, ond *O* / hu
	30.13	**numquid**
359	29.18	nalles *C*, nales *O* / na
	30.13	**non**
360	29.18	gað / farað
	30.14	**ite**
361	29.20	mænnene (menn *O*) ... nunnan / þeowene
	30.14	**ancilla**
362	29.21	nearolice *C*, nioroglice *O* / angsumlice
	30.14	**anxietate**
363	29.23	sorgian / beo ... carfulle
	30.15	**esse solliciti**
364	29.25	winnende / swincende
	30.16	**laboratura**
365	29.26	biddeþ *C*, bædeð *O* / gyrneð
	30.16	**quaesitura**
366	29.27	cyrde / gecyrde
	30.18	**-gressus**
367	29.29	ongæt *C*, ongeat *O* / oncneow
	30.19	**agnovit**
368	30.2	bysene *C*, bysne *O* / gebysnunge
	30.20	**exemplum**
369	30.5	anes / sumes
370	30.5	rices mannes (monnes *O*) / undercininges
	30.21	**reguli**
371	30.6	fram *C*, from *O* / þurh
372	30.7	hæle gæfe *C*, hælo agefe *O* / gehælenne
	30.22	**restituit saluti**
373	30.11	eft ... seald (geseald *O*) / forgifen
	30.22	**restitutum**
374	30.14	gehaten / behaten
375	30.14	witodlice *C*, weotodlice *O* / eornostlice
	30.24	**autem**
376	30.19	cwæð *C*, *def. O* / sæde
	30.25	**dixit**
377	30.22	hwæþre *C*, *def. O* / swaþeah
	31.2	**tamen**
378	30.22	nænigne *C*, [ ]nine *O* / nænne
	31.2	**quempiam**
379	30.24	se *C*, *def. O* / he
	31.2	**qui**
380	30.24	medmycclum *C*, medmiclum *O* / lytlum
	31.2	**non ... longum**
381	30.33	þa / 7
382	31.3	gefeoll / afeoll
	31.7	**cecidit**
383	31.4	geswenced *C*, geswencedu *O* / gedreht
	31.8	**vexaretur**
384	31.4	hrædlice / hraðe
	31.8	**sub celeritate**
385	31.6	þis / hit
386	31.6	sædon *C*, sægdon *O* / gecyðed
	31.8	**nuntiatum**
387	31.7	hraðe *C*, raðe *O* / ofstlice
	31.9	**concitus**
388	31.9	gehælde / gehulpe
	31.9	**concurrerit; sucurreret** *Bo*, **protegeret** *Maurists, var.*
389	31.10	swa / þa
	31.9	*om.;* **ut** *C*
390	31.11	eode / agan
	31.10	**-gressus**
391	31.13	swencte / gegrap
	31.11	**arripuerat**
392	31.19	æbylignysse *C*, æbylgnesse *O* / yrsunge
	31.13	**indignatione**
393	31.20	of / fram
	31.14	**ab-; dis-** Pa_2

390 Hecht printed *ineode* and *inn agan.*

394 31.21 stowe ... wunede (gewunade *O*) / wunungstowe
31.14 **locum**
395 31.22 fæmnan *C, om. O* / þeowene
31.14 **famulam**
396 31.23 þa sona / þærrihte
31.15 **protinus**
397 31.24 onufan þæt / syððan
31.15 **ultra**
398 31.25 gehrinan / æthrinan
31.15 **contingere**
399 31.29 fæder / wer
31.17 **viro** *M;* **vir** *S*
400 31.30 hlaford / fæder
31.18 **pater**
401 31.31 se / þe
31.18 **qui**
402 32.6 bebod *C,* [ ]od *O* / lare
403 32.7 cyþde 7 lærde / bodode
31.21 **praedicare**
404 32.8 gesohte / ferde ... to
31.22 **adiit; suadit** W_2
405 32.9 byldo / dyrstinysse
31.21 **ausu**
406 32.10 bealdlice *C,* baldlice *O* / openlice
407 32.15 eardast / wunast
32.1 **degis; legis** *La*
408 32.15 wæs / wearð
409 32.16 geþread 7 genyded / geneadod
32.2 **conpulsus**
410 32.18 secgan / asæde
32.3 **indicavit**
411 32.20 wisan / þing
32.4 **ea**
412 32.22 gemunde / on ... mode ... smeade
32.4 **mecum ... pertracto**
413 32.23 geong man *C,* giong mon *O* / iungling
32.5 **iuvenis**
414 32.25 7 / þa
32.6 **adque** *M*
415 32.25 he / se
416 32.25 læceiren / blodseax
32.6 **medicinalem ferramentum ... flebothomum** (*C;* **fleugodiomum** *as a gloss* Pa_2)
417 32.27 geseoh / efne
32.7 **ecce**
418 32.27 sette / asette
32.7 **posui**
419 32.28 ac / nu
420 32.28 gang / far
32.8 **egredere**
421 32.29 æfter / of
32.8 **ex**
422 32.30 godcundra / godes
32.9 **deo**
423 32.32 þæs / þises
32.10 **huius**
424 32.34 witan 7 ongytan (ongitan *O*) / oncnawan
32.10 **agnoscere; cognoscere** *Ta*
425 33.2 7swarode / to cwæð
426 33.4 nalles *C,* nallæs *O* / na
32.12 **non**
427 33.7 naht *C,* noht *O* / nan þing
428 33.8 gyfen *C,* gifen *O* / forgifen
429 33.8 ac symble / witodlice
32.13 **quippe**
430 33.9 gaþ / stæppað
32.14 **-veniunt**
431 33.9 beforan / fore
32.14 **prae-**
432 33.12 geweaxen 7 gemærsien (gemersien *O*) / weaxan
32.15 **succrescunt**
433 33.13 hwæþre / swaþeah
32.15 **tamen**
434 33.13 7gites / oncnawennysse
32.15 **cognitione**
435 33.14 þisses *C,* þises *O* / þæs
32.15 **eius**
436 33.15 ongæt *C,* ongeat *O* / cuðe
32.17 **agnovit; cognovit** V_1
437 33.15 eadiga / arwurða
32.16 **reverentissimus; bonus ac reverentissimus** V_3
438 33.20 þæs / his

402 Hecht reported *O* as defective. **403** Hecht reported *[ ]de 7 lærde* for *O*. **407** Hecht printed *underwunast* for *H*, beside *CO*'s *under ... eardast*. **430** Hecht printed *forestæppað* for *H*, beside *CO*'s *gaþ ... beforan*. **434** Hecht reported *ondgites* for *O*.

439	33.21	þa þa / þonne
	32.18	**quando**
440	33.22	gehwæþrede *C*, geðwærlæhte *O* / geþwærode
	32.18	**concordabat**
441	33.22	geornfulnesse / bigenge
	32.19	**studio**
442	33.23	7 *C*, *om. O* / eornostlice
	32.19	**quippe**
443	33.23	swiþe / swa
	32.19	**tantus**
444	33.24	ege / hæte
	32.20	**fervor**
445	33.27	heold / wæs ... hyrde
	32.20	**praeesset**
446	33.28	þurh / on
	32.21	**per**
447	33.28	cristenra (cristðenra *O*) folca gesomnunge / cyrcean
	32.21	**aecclesias** *M*
448	33.30	þurh / geond
	32.21	**per**
449	34.1	yfellic *C*, yfelic *O* / waclic
	33.3	**vilis**
450	34.1	gegerelan / gewædum
	33.3	**vestibus**
451	34.5	se / he
452	34.6	forhogode *C*, *om. O* / forsewen
	33.4	**dispiceret**
453	34.6	togenes *C*, *om. O* / ongean
	33.4	**re-**
454	34.7	faran *C*, færan *O* / feran
	33.5	**tendebat**
455	34.10	forcuþlocost *C*, forcuðlucust *O* / forcuðost
	33.6	**dispicabilius**
456	34.12	bridelse / bridele
	33.7	**freno**
457	34.15	alegd / ahangene
	33.9	**missos**
458	34.18	com / becom
	33.10	**pervenisset**
459	34.18	ontynde / geopenode
	33.10	**aperiebat**
460	34.19	æspryng *C*, æsprencg *O* / wyllspring
	33.10	**fontem**
461	34.19	godcundra / haligra
462	34.26	byð *C*, bið *O* / gewuna is
	33.12	**est; assolet** V_3, **solet** *Cl*
463	34.27	leasolecendra / liffetendra
	33.12	**adulantium**
464	34.27	cweleþ 7 swenceþ / cwylmeð
	33.13	**necans; nectit** V_3
465	34.29	lysteþ / wyle
	33.13	**amplectendo**
466	34.29	tid *C*, tiid *O* / timan
	33.13	**tempore**
467	34.33	olæcende *C*, oliciende *O* / liffetende
	33.14	**adulando; fraudulenter** *as a gloss La*
468	35.1	seofiende *C*, siofiende *O* / syrwdon
	33.14	**quaesti; accusatores** *as a gloss La*
469	35.2	ceorlisca wer / ceorl
	33.15	**vir** (*om. M*) **rusticus**
470	35.4	neþeþ *C*, deð *O* / gedyrstlæcð
	33.17	**praesumpsit**
471	35.5	agnað / geagnað
	33.17	**usurpare; contaminare** *as a gloss La*
472	35.9	se / þe
	33.18	**qui**
473	35.10	ongytan *C*, ongietan *O* / oncnawe
	33.19	**agnuscat** *M*
474	35.12	þa / soðlice
	33.19	**autem**
475	35.12	sona / swa
	33.19	**sic-**
476	35.15	olehtung *C*, olehtuncg *O* / liffetung
	33.20	**adulatio**
477	35.17	æmtignesse / inngange
	33.20	**ostio; hostio** V_3, **hospitio** *Ta*
478	35.19	moste / sceolde
	33.22	**debuissit** *M*
479	35.21	ongæte *C*, ongeate *O* / oncneowe
	33.23	**cognuscerit** *M*
480	35.22	7 *C*, ond *O* / þærto
	33.23	**tamen**
481	35.22	sænde *C*, sende *O* / asende
	34.1	**mittens**
482	35.23	æfter þon / eft syððan
	34.1	**postmodum**

483	35.25	gelædde / lædde
	34.3	**deduceret**
484	35.26	are / wyrðmynde
	34.2	**honore**
485	35.26	þeow / wer
	34.3	**famulus**
486	35.27	oht *C, def. O* / æni þing
	34.3	**quicquam**
487	35.27	gemetingce *C*, gemetincge *O* / gemittinge
	34.3	**conventione; convectione** *as a gloss Ta*
488	35.29	wisan *C*, wi[ ] *O* / þingum
	34.4	**eo**
489	36.2	heig *C*, heg *O* / gærs
	34.7	**faenum** *M*
490	36.5	oferhigdigne *C*, oferhygdigne *O* / ofermodine
	34.8	**superbum**
491	36.7	þisne / þone
	34.9	**hunc**
492	36.10	gehigde *C*, gehygde *O* / mode
	34.11	**spiritu**
493	36.11	eode / stop
	34.11	**-gressus**
494	36.15	geacsode *C*, geascode *O* / gehyrde
	35.1	**audivit**
495	36.17	unmætum *C*, unmæte *O* / ormætum
	35.2	**inmenso**
496	36.26	7 *C*, ond *O* / hwæt
497	36.27	gehalette *C*, gehaletæ *O* / gehælde
	35.6	**resalutato**
498	36.29	hig *C*, heg *O* / gærs
	35.6	**faenum**
499	37.3	to ... cyrrende / ongean yrnendne
	35.10	**revertentem**
500	37.4	hig / gærs
	35.11	**faenum**
501	37.8	wende / sende
	35.13	**misi**
502	37.9	lædan / gelædan
	35.13	**deducere; ducere** *changed to* **deducere** *Hf*
503	37.9	heig *C*, hig *O* / gærs
	35.13	**faenum**
504	37.13	gehammenum *C*, behammenum *O* / geclutedum
	35.15	**clavatis**
505	37.15	gangende *C*, gongende *O* / wæs ... þyderweard
	35.16	**positum**
506	37.17	þa semninga (samninga *O*) ... swa / midþam þe
	35.18	**viro (*M*) ... repente ut**
507	37.20	gegerelan *C*, gegirelan *O* / gyrelan
	35.18	**habitu**
508	37.20	þohte / smeade
	35.19	**praeparabat; meditabat** *M*
509	37.20	þwerum *C*, ðweore *O* / toþundenum
	35.19	**proterva**
510	37.21	on ... oferhigdum / þwyrlicost
511	37.22	to *C, om. O* / wið
	35.19	**al-; ad-** *La*
512	37.24	wæs neah *C*, neah æt wæs *O* / nealæhte
	35.20	**comminus (prope** *as a gloss La*) **adfuit**
513	37.25	unaræfnedlicu *C*, unaræfnigendlicu *O* / unacumendlic
	35.21	**intolerabilis**
514	37.25	fyrhtu / forhtnys
	35.21	**pavor**
515	37.26	uneaðe / earfoðlice
	35.22	**vix**
516	37.27	genihtsumian / hæfde ... geweald
	35.22	**sufficere**
517	37.28	sæde *C*, asægde *O* / abeodan
	35.22	**insinuandum**
518	37.30	geeadmodadum *C*, eaðmode *O* / geeaðmedum
	35.23	**humiliato**
519	37.30	gaste / mode
	35.23	**spiritu**
520	37.30	georne / arn

499 Hecht reported *yrnende* for *H*. **511** Hecht printed *to sprecan* and *wiðsprecan*. **518** Hecht reported *eadmode* for *O*.

	35.23	**cucurrit**
521	38.1	for *C*, *om.* *O* / fore
	35.24	**pro**
522	38.4	don ... þancas (þoncas *O*) / þancienne
	36.2	**gratias ... agere**
523	38.4	unmæte / ormætlice
	36.2	**inmensas**
524	38.6	sæde *C*, sægde *O* / cwæð
	36.2	**asserens**
525	38.7	hean / healican
	36.3	**summum**
526	38.8	þa hraðe (raðe *O*) / þærrihte
	36.3	**ilico**
527	38.10	beon / wurdon
528	38.12	geferan / ærendracan
	36.5	**executorem**
529	38.12	swiðe / þearle
	36.5	**vehementissime; vehementer** Pa_2
530	38.13	on (...) tid / huruþinga hrædlice
	36.5	**statim**
531	38.13	utfaran *C*, utgan *O* / feran
	36.6	**exire**
532	38.15	nænigra (nænig *O*) þinga / natoþæshwon
	36.6	**nullatenus**
533	38.16	swiþe / to þam
534	38.20	þonne / nu
535	38.21	on þysum ylcan dæge *C*, þis ilcan dæge *O* / nu todæg
	36.8	**hodierna die**
536	38.23	færeld ... þurhteoð *C*, færld ... ðurhtihð *O* / farað
	36.9	**eximus**
537	38.23	7 (ond *O*) ... swa / witodlice
	36.9	**itaque**
538	38.24	wæs / wearð
539	38.24	genyded / geneadod
	36.10	**coactus; compulsus** O_2
540	38.24	fram *C*, for *O* / mid
541	38.27	þa / efne þæs
	36.11	**cum ecce**
542	38.27	æfterfylgendan (æftran fylgendan *O*) dæge / morgen
	36.11	**sequenti die**
543	38.28	ærendraca / cniht
	36.12	**puer**
544	38.29	epistolan *C*, epistole *O* / ærendgewrite
	36.12	**epistola**
545	38.31	epistolan *C*, epistole *O* / write
	36.12	**[epistola]**
546	38.33	aht *C*, oht *O* / ænig þing
547	38.33	grette *C*, grete *O* / hrepode
	36.13	**contingere**
548	39.3	ongæt *C*, ongeat *O* / sæde
	36.15	**cognovit**
549	39.6	sænded *C*, sended *O* / asended
	36.15	**missus**
550	39.6	apostolica biscop (bisceop *O*) / healica papa
	36.16	**pontifex**
551	39.7	wæs / wearð
	36.16	**fuerat**
552	39.7	abreged / gebreged
	36.16	**exterritus**
553	39.8	forhwon / hu
	36.16	**cur** *C*
554	39.11	spanan / gelangian
	36.17	**exhibendum**
555	39.11	hraðe *C*, raðe *O* / þærrihte
	36.17	**protinus**
556	39.16	swencan *C*, swencean *O* / geswencean
	36.19	**fatigari**
557	39.16	siþ / weg
558	39.18	wæs / wearð
559	39.18	geunrotsod *C*, geunrosad *O* / unrot
	36.20	**contristatus**
560	39.20	þa sona / þærrihte
	36.21	**statim**
561	39.21	nu / syððan
	36.21	**iam**
562	39.24	hwylcnehugu *C*, hwylcnehwega *O* / sume
	36.22	**aliquantulum**
563	39.25	fyrst / hwile
564	39.26	genyddum / geneadodum
	36.23	**coacto**

542 Hecht printed *æftranfylgendan*. **545** Both versions of the translation render *epistola* twice, at 38.29 and 38.31.

565 39.27 hwæthugu *C*, hwæthwega *O* / sume

566 39.28 gewinnes / geswinces
36.23 **laboris**

567 39.28 ongyt *C*, ongit *O* / oncnaw
36.24 **cognusce** *M*

568 39.30 hyrnysse *C*, heordnysse *O* / gehyrdnysse
36.24 **custodia**

569 39.33 are / wyrðmynde
36.26 **honore**

570 40.1 scamiað *C*, scomiað *O* / forsceamiað
37.1 **erubiscunt**

571 40.1 syn *C*, sin *O* / beon
36.26 **esse**

572 40.2 wið þan (þon *O*) / þærongean
37.1 **contra; e contra** *C*, **contrario** Pa_1

573 40.4 aþindað 7 aswellað / toþindað
37.3 **tument**

574 40.8 soðfæstnys (soðfæstnes *O*) ... Crist / hælend
37.3 **veritas**

575 40.10 godiaþ *C*, *om. O* / rihtwisiað
37.3 **iustificatis** *C*

576 40.13 byþ *C*, bið *O* / is
37.5 **est**

577 40.15 swyþe *C*, swiðe *O* / forswiðe
37.7 **valde**

578 40.18 deofollice / lease

579 40.18 scinnys ... olehtinga *C*, scyndnes ... olehtunga *O* / liffetung

580 40.20 7swarode / to cwæð

581 40.20 tohwan / hwæt
37.9 **quid**

582 40.22 fuloft / foroft

583 40.24 aleah *C*, abeah *O* / gewat
37.10 **-cedit**

584 40.31 þonne hwæþre (wæðre *O*) / þeahhwæðere
37.12 **tamen**

585 41.1 hwæþre / swaþeah
37.14 **tamen**

586 41.2 geseon ne geþæncan (geðencean *O*) / oncnawan
37.14 **videmus**

587 41.5 syn *C*, sin *O* / beon

588 41.7 ac / soðlice
37.16 **vero**

589 41.10 forhergod / awesteð
37.17 **devastat**

590 41.11 woruldlicra ymbhogena *C*, woroldlicra embehogena *O* / woruldcara
37.17 **curarum**

591 41.13 wisum *C*, wison *O* / þingum

592 41.14 medmare / læsse
37.18 **minor**

593 41.14 hwylcum *C*, hwilcum *O* / gehwilcum anum

594 41.16 ma / swyðor
37.19 **tanto-**

595 41.17 hwylcumhugu *C*, hwilcum-hwega *O* / gehwilcum
37.19 **qualibet**

596 41.20 wisum *C*, wison *O* / þingum
37.19 **re**

597 41.24 7swarode / cwæð

598 41.26 ongæt *C*, ongeat *O* / oncneow
37.23 **cocognovi; agnovi** *Maurists*

599 41.27 þam ylcan (ilcan *O*) / þisum
37.22 **hoc**

600 41.31 eode / com

601 42.3 geþohte / asmeade
38.3 **perpendere**

602 42.4 arwurðe *C*, arwurða *O* / mære
38.3 **qualis-**

603 42.5 semninga *C*, samninga *O* / færinga
38.4 **repente**

604 42.6 he / se

605 42.9 þon (ðam *O*) þe / þærþær
38.4 **illic**

606 42.9 on stod ... on (*def. O*) ... stede (stealle *O*) / gesette
38.4 **in ... stabilitate**

607 42.13 ongæton *C*, ongeato[ ] *O* / oncneowon
38.6 **cognuscerent** *M;* **agnoscerent** V_1

608 42.18 word *C*, w[ ] *O* / þing

579 Hecht reported *olehtinga* for *O*. **581** The rubricator of *O* supplied the letter *h*. **602** Hecht reported *ar[ ]* for *O*. **607** Hecht reported *ongeat[ ]* for *O*.

	38.8	**ea**
609	42.18	her / herto
	38.8	**sub-**
610	42.19	secgcan ***C***, secgan ***O*** / geþeode
	38.8	**[sub]iungo**
611	42.22	licaþ / gelicode
	38.9	**placet; prefertur** *as a gloss* Be_2
612	42.23	sæde ***C***, sægde ***O*** / rehte
613	42.27	geflugon ***C***, gefulgon ***O*** / flugon
	38.12	**fugierunt**
614	42.27	in / into
	38.11	**in**
615	42.29	todrifon / astencton
	38.14	**discuterent**
616	42.29	þurh / mid
	38.14	**per**
617	42.30	7 eac / oððe
	38.14	**aut**
618	42.33	grimman ***C***, grimme ***O*** / teartum
	38.15	**acri**
619	43.1	loca nu ***C***, loca nu la ***O*** / eala
	38.16	**e; o *Hf*, eu** W_2**, heu heu *Maurists***
620	43.3	scyldan / bewerast
	38.17	**defendas**
621	43.4	sona / þa hrædlice
	38.17	**protinus**
622	43.6	urnon / ahruron
	38.18	**corruentes**
623	43.6	geond / on
	38.18	**in**
624	43.7	land / eorðan
	39.1	**terra**
625	43.8	wæron / wurdon
	39.1	**sunt**
626	43.11	nohte ***C***, noht ***O*** / na leng
	39.3	**non**
627	43.11	gretan / dyrstilice hreppan
	39.2	**temerare**
628	43.13	mundbyrde / bewerede
	39.4	**defendit**
629	43.14	þegnas / gingran
	39.3	**discipulos**
630	43.16	mundbyrd / frið
	39.4	**remedium**
631	43.16	æfter þon / syððon
	39.4	**post**
632	43.16	geflugon / flugon
	39.4	**fugientibus**
633	43.20	7 (ond ***O***) eac / soþlice
634	43.22	þæs / sumes
	39.5	**cuiusdam**
635	43.23	þe / se
	39.6	**qui *C***
636	43.25	leofde ***C***, lædde ***O*** / adreah
	39.8	**duxit**
637	43.26	ungneþelice / unheanlice
	39.7	**non mediocriter**
638	43.27	be þam / eac
	39.8	**etiam**
639	43.27	manige ***C***, monige ***O*** / sume
	39.8	**quidam**
640	43.27	on ***C***, in ***O*** / of
	39.9	**ex**
641	43.33	man ***C***, mon ***O*** / wer
	39.11	**vir**
642	44.3	gemærsode / gewidmærode
	39.13	**tetenderat**
643	44.5	cyþnesse / cyððe
	39.12	**notitiam**
644	44.6	eallinga / eallunga
	39.13	**funditus**
645	44.7	geornnysse ***C***, geornesse ***O*** / geornfullnysse
	40.1	**adnisu; nisu *Cl***
646	44.10	eles wana / elewana
	40.2	**oleum de-**
647	44.10	þes / se
648	44.14	tapor / weocon
	40.5	**papirum**
649	44.18	ongyt / understand
	40.6	**perpende**
650	44.20	mid nyode (nede ***O***) genyded / geneadod
	40.7	**necessitate conpulsus**
651	44.22	gewænde ***C***, gewende ***O*** / awennde
	40.8	**mutavit**
652	44.27	man ***C***, mon ***O*** / wer
653	44.30	7swarode / to cwæð
654	45.1	dyde / worhte
655	45.5	oferhigd ***C***, oferhygd ***O*** /

610 Both *her ... secg(c)an* and *herto ... geþeode* correspond to *subiungo*.

upahafennysse
656 45.5 oht *C*, aht *O* / ænig þing
40.14 **quae**
657 45.9 gedyde / worhte
40.15 **fecit**
658 45.10 ongytest / oncnæwst
40.15 **agnuscis** *M*
659 45.10 hraðe *C*, raðe *O* / sona
40.15 **citius**
660 45.13 dæda / weorces
40.16 **facti**
661 45.14 get *C*, git *O* / eac
40.17 **etiam**
662 45.14 hwæthugu / sum þing
40.17 [**etiam**]
663 45.15 lære / secge
40.17 **aedifices**
664 45.19 7swarode / to cwæð
665 45.21 manige *C*, monige *O* / fela
40.19 **multi**
666 45.23 boldgetalum / scirum
40.19 **provinciis; provinciae partibus** O_2
667 45.27 fylde / gefyllde
40.22 **reficiendis**
668 46.4 getæht *C*, geteaht *O* / ætywed
41.1 **ostendi**
669 46.7 dysigan / stuntan
41.2 **stultae**
670 46.8 geearnung *C*, geearnuncg *O* / earnung
41.3 **meritum**
671 46.9 sy *C*, sie *O* / beo
672 46.9 swylce / of
41.3 **ex**
673 46.10 ansyn *C*, onsien *O* / missenlicnysse
41.3 **qualitate**
674 46.13 nolde / ongan
41.4 **coepit**
675 46.13 gelyfan / beon ... ungeleaf
41.5 **credere**
676 46.14 he (ðæt *O*) se ylca / he hit
41.4 **ipsum (ipse** *La*) **hunc**
677 46.17 þæt / þær
678 46.18 bysmrung *C*, bismruncg *O* / sacu
41.6 **rixa**
679 46.21 næfre / na
41.7 **non**
680 46.22 haligdomes / halinysse
681 46.28 naht *C*, noht *O* / nan þing
41.10 **nihil**
682 46.29 þæt / þis
41.10 **quod**
683 46.31 rædde 7 fylde / behwearf
41.11 **reficiebat**
684 46.32 hraðe / hrædlice
41.12 **concitus**
685 46.32 ofdune / nyðer
41.12 **di-; de-** *Bo*
686 47.1 gefeoll on ... clyppinge / beclypte
41.12 **in ... amplexum ruit**
687 47.3 teon (teo[ ] *O*) to / clyppan
41.13 **constringere**
688 47.3 be / mid
689 47.4 þancas ... sæde *C*, ðoncas ... sægde *O* / þancian
41.14 **gratias agere**
690 50.13 to / æt
691 50.13 utancumenum *C*, utoncundum *O* / utlendisceum
46.9 **extraneis**
692 50.14 hwæthugu / sumne dæl
46.10 **aliquantulum**
693 50.20 þæt / hit
694 50.21 broðra *C*, broðro *O* / gebroðru
46.12 **fratres**
695 50.24 hwylcne *C*, hwelcne *O* / sume
696 50.24 æfwyrdlan *C*, æwyrdlan *O* / hynða
46.13 **damna**
697 50.25 geþrowedon *C*, geðrowodon *O* / þoledon
46.14 **paterentur**
698 50.29 gesomnian / gegaderian
46.15 **collegi**
699 50.30 bydene / eletreddan
46.15 **praelo**

662 Both *get* and *hwæthugu*, or *eac* and *sum þing*, may render *etiam*. 665 Hecht did not make out *O*'s reading. 670 Hecht reported *ærnung* for *H*. 676 Hecht reported *ðæ* for *O*. 682 Hecht reported *þæ* for *O*. 683 Hecht reported *bewhearf* for *H*.

700	50.34	7 / þa
	47.2	**-que**
701	50.34	þæt / hit
702	50.34	wæs / wearð
	47.2	**est**
703	51.1	broðra *C*, broðro *O* / gebroðru
	47.2	**fratres**
704	51.2	hwylcnehugu / sumne dæl
705	51.2	medmycclum *C*, medmiclum *O* / lytlum
	47.2	**parvolo; parvo** O_2
706	51.7	þam oþrum / him
707	51.9	æfter þan (þon *O*) / syððon
	47.4	**postmodum**
708	51.9	gecigde *C*, gecegde *O* / gelangode
	47.4	**accitis; accersitis** V_2
709	51.9	broðru *C*, broðro *O* / gebroðru
	47.5	**fratribus**
710	51.14	to þon / swa
	47.6	**quatinus**
711	51.17	fætelsas / fatu
	47.7	*om.;* **vasa** *Hf*
712	51.19	7 (ond *O*) þa / soþlice
	47.8	**vero**
713	51.21	fore / for
714	51.23	ælce dæge *C*, *def. O* / dæghwamlice
	47.10	**cottidie** *M*
715	51.24	soþfæstnysse (soðfæstnesse *O*) ... Crist ... godes sunu / soðfæstan hælendes
	47.10	**veritatis**
716	51.27	se / þe
	47.10	**quae**
717	51.32	7swarode *C*, 7swarede *O* / cwæð
718	51.33	tid *C*, tiid *O* / timan
	47.12	**tempore**
719	52.2	sæde *C*, sægde *O* / dyde
	47.13	**feci**
720	52.5	stihtigendum *C*, stiehtiendum *O* / under ... anwealde
	47.14	**auctore**
721	52.10	ær beforan / bufan ymbe
	47.16	**prae-**
722	52.11	haten / geciged
	47.16	**vocatur**
723	52.12	gelædde / adreah
	47.17	**duxit**
724	52.13	manegum *C*, monigum *O* / halgum
	47.17	**sanctis**
725	52.15	7 *C*, *om. O* / witodlice
	47.18	**videlicet**
726	52.16	unmæte / ormæte
	47.18	**ingens**
727	52.16	stanclif *C*, stancliif *O* / stanclud
	47.19	**rupis** *M;* **ripis** *A*
728	52.18	þa / soðlice
	47.20	**viro** *M*
729	52.20	gewin / geswinc
	47.21	**labores**
730	52.20	geedleanode / geleanienne
	47.21	**remunerare**
731	52.22	clife / clude
	47.21	**rupe**
732	52.23	geworden *C*, gewordenu *O* / gehyred
	47.22	**facta**
733	52.24	swa / þus
734	52.24	gecleopode *C*, gecliopade *O* / clypode
	47.22	**clamaret**
735	52.26	wæron / wurdon
	47.23	**sunt**
736	52.27	ane / swiðe
737	52.28	berhtmhwile *C*, bærhtmhwile *O* / lytle hwile
	48.1	**parvo ... momento**
738	52.28	aswygode *C*, ætswigde *O* / geswigode
	48.1	**siluit**
739	52.29	þyder *C*, ðider *O* / þær
	48.1	**e-**
740	52.29	onsænded *C*, onsended *O* / clypode
	48.1	**-missa**
741	52.30	midþy þa *C*, mitty ðe *O* / þa þa
	48.2	**dum**
742	52.33	nænig / nan
	48.3	**non**
743	52.33	tweo *C*, twy *O* / twynung
	48.3	**dubium**
744	52.34	forðfore / forðsið
	48.3	**obitus**

745	53.1	þa / witodlice
	48.4	**igitur**
746	53.1	ymb ***C***, embe ***O*** / binnan
	48.4	**intra**
747	53.2	geferde ***C***, gewat ***O*** / forðferde
748	53.3	of lichaman (lichoman ***O***) gelædde / forðferdon
	48.5	**ex carne (corpore *Ta*) educti (ducti *changed to* educti *Sa*)**
749	53.7	æt / to
	48.6	**ad**
750	53.7	cigingce ***C***, cigynne ***O*** / gecigednysse
	48.7	**vocandum**
751	53.8	hwæthugu ***C***, æthugu ***O*** / sume hwile
	48.7	**parum; parvum *La***
752	53.11	he / se
753	53.13	gecyþed / geswutelod
	48.9	**monstraretur; demonstraretur *Cl***
754	53.15	medmycelne ***C***, mid mycelre ***O*** / lyttlan
	48.9	**parvum; parum *Bo***
755	53.19	wise / þing
	48.10	**res**
756	53.20	utferde (utfærde ***O***) of (...) lichaman / forðferde
	48.11	**de corpore exiret (*C*)**
757	53.22	ofer / æfter
	48.12	**super; post *as a gloss La***
758	53.28	ofer / æfter
	48.14	**super**
759	53.28	middanearde / middangearde
	48.14	**mundo; seculo V_3**
760	53.31	þonne hwæþre / swaþeah
	48.15	**tamen**
761	53.34	gecyþed / geswutelod
	48.16	**clariscerit *M***
762	54.4	hwæþre / swaþeah
	48.20	**tamen**
763	54.5	getogen / atogen
	48.20	**subtractus**
764	54.5	leohte / life
	48.20	**luce**
765	54.6	geþingum / þingungum
	48.20	**intercessionibus**
766	54.7	ærest / elles
	48.21	**aliud**
767	54.8	nemne ***C***, nimðe ***O*** / buton
	48.21	**nisi**
768	54.9	beoð / synd
	48.22	**sunt**
769	54.9	drihtene ***C***, drihtne ***O*** / gode
	48.22	**dominum; deum O_2**
770	54.13	nænigra (nænige ***O***) þinga / toþæshwon
	48.24	**nequaquam**
771	54.20	þus / swa
	49.1	**ita**
772	54.22	mid / of
	49.2	**ex**
773	54.22	gewinne / geswince
	49.2	**labore**
774	54.23	þissum ***C***, þisum ***O*** / þam
	49.2	**hoc**
775	54.25	geteohhode ***C***, getihgode ***O*** / gedihtnode
	49.4	**disposuit**
776	54.26	onfonne ***C***, gifanne ***O*** / forgifenne
	49.4	**donare**
777	55.1	þu / la
778	55.3	7 / gewisslice
	49.8	**certe etenim**
779	55.8	þam ylcan (ilcan ***O***) / him
	49.10	**cui**
780	55.8	gehet / behet
	49.10	**promisit**
781	55.9	bletsige / gebledsige
	49.11	**benedicam**
782	55.9	gemænifealde ***C***, gemonifealde ***O*** / gemenigfylde
	49.11	**multiplicabo**
783†	55.13	wisan / þinge
	49.13	**re**
784	55.16	gemanifealdigum ***C***, gemonigfealdan ***O*** / gemenifyldan
	49.13	**multiplicare**
785	55.17	hwæþre swa swa / swaþeah
	49.14	**tamen**
786	55.23	forþon / eornostlice
	49.17	**ergo**

784 Hecht reported *gemonifealdan* for *O*.

787 55.25 forhwan *C*, forhwon *O* / hwi
49.18 **quur**
788 55.25 elles / þonne
789 55.25 onfeng / underfeng
49.18 **accepit**
790† 55.33 gemanigfealdod *C*, gemonigfaldad *O* / gemenifyldenne
49.20 **multiplicari**
791† 55.34 naht æniges *C*, noht ænigre *O* / nan
49.22 **nihil**
792† 56.1 þissere *C*, ðisse *O* / þam
793† 56.1 fore / nu
794† 56.2 sprecenan *C*, spræcenane *O* / sædest
795† 56.2 wisan / þingum
796† 56.3 ontynde / geopenode
49.22 **aperuit**
797† 56.4 gesægene *C*, gesegne *O* / segene
798† 56.5 7swarode / cwæð
799† 56.6 hwæthugu *C*, hwæthwega *O* / sum þing
50.1 **aliquid**
800† 56.7 ongyte *C*, ongite *O* / oncnawe
50.2 **cognuscas** *M*
801 56.10 cyðnysse *C*, cyðnesse *O* / cyððe
50.3 **notitiae**
802 56.12 gemete / mægene
50.4 **-modo**
803 56.14 7swarode *C*, 7swarode 7 sægde *O* / to cwæð
804 56.17 biscopdom *C*, [ ]sceopdom *O* / bisceophad
50.6 **episcopatum officio**
805 56.18 haten / genemned
50.6 **dicitur**
806 56.20 rihtlice / wel
807 56.22 sæde *C*, sægde *O* / rehte
50.8 **narrat**
808† 56.22 se / þe
50.8 **qui**
809† 56.26 ma / swa ... oftor
50.10 **quanto**
810† 56.31 wædl / wædlung
50.11 **paupertas**
811† 56.31 þearfednes / hafenleast
50.11 [**paupertas**]
812† 57.1 naht *C*, noht *O* / nan þing
50.12 **nihil-**
813† 57.4 wæs / wearð
50.14 **est**
814† 57.5 forslagan *C*, forslegen *O* / forðorcean
50.14 **vastata**
815† 57.5 forhergod *C*, forhergad *O* / awæstod
50.14 [**vastata**]
816† 57.9 geclystru / clistrum
50.15 **racimi**
817 57.13 sæde ... þancas *C*, sægde ... ðoncas *O* / þancode
50.17 **gratias retulit**
818 57.14 þæt / forþam þe
50.17 **quia**
819 57.15 ongæt *C*, ongeat *O* / oncneow
50.18 **cognovit**
820 57.16 ma / swyðor
821 57.16 geswæncan 7 genyrwian *C*, geswencean 7 genyrwan *O* / geangsumod
50.18 **angustari; angustiari** V_2
822 57.18 tid / tima
50.18 **tempus**
823 57.21 weard / hyrde
51.1 **custodem**
824 57.24 geornlice *C*, geornlicre *O* / carfullre
51.1 **sollerti**
825 57.24 wacunge *C*, wacone *O* / wæccean
51.1 **vigilantia**
826 57.28 bydenu *C*, bydena *O* / kyfa
51.4 **dolea**
827 57.29 gewuna / gewunelic
51.4 **consueverat**

793† and **794†** Hecht printed *foresprecenan* and *nu sædest.* **802** Hecht reported *ge[ ]* for *O*.
811† Both *wædl* and *þearfednes*, or *wædlung* and *hafenleast*, render *paupertas.* **815†** For *H's halgode 7 awæstod* read, with Hecht, *hagole 7 awæstod*, beside *7 forhergod ... hægle (hagle* O*)* in the original translation. Both *forslagan* and *forhergod*, or *forðorcean* and *awæstod*, render *vastata.* **818** *C* abbreviates *ꝥ*.
821 Hecht reported *geswæncean* for *O*.

No.	Ref.	Gloss / Lemma
828†	57.31	hit / þæt
	51.5	**quod**
829†	57.33	þohte / wende
830†	58.1	ungewittignesse *C*, ungewittignes *O* / on unwis
	51.6	**insana; insania** *Bo*
831†	58.3	nænig / nan
	51.7	**menime**
832†	58.4	þehhwæþre *C*, ðonne hwæðre *O* / swaþeah
	51.7	**tamen**
833†	58.7	hyrde / gehyrsumode
	51.8	**obtemperans**
834†	58.8	fatu / winfatu
835†	58.8	swa / æfter
	51.8	**ex**
836†	58.9	ac *C*, ond *O* / hwæt
837†	58.10	gesomnode *C*, gesamnode *O* / gegaderode
	51.10	**collegit**
838†	58.11	geclystru / clystru
	51.9	**racimos**
839†	58.13	buton / 7
	51.11	**-que**
840	58.14	cnihte / cnapan
	51.11	**puerolo**
841	58.15	cniht / cnapan
	51.11	**[puerolo]**
842	58.17	wringan / tredan
	51.12	**calcari**
843	58.19	geclystrum / clystrum
	51.13	**racimis**
844	58.19	aþyde / fleow
	51.14	**-fluerit** *M*
845	58.20	dæl *C*, del *O* / hwæt
	51.13	**aliquid**
846	58.21	nyman *C*, neoman *O* / underfon
	51.15	**suscepere**
847	58.22	mid *C*, fore *O* / for
	51.16	**pro**
848	58.23	bydena / kyfa
	51.15	**dolea**
849	58.25	þeh þe *C*, ða ðe *O* / þæt
	51.16	**ut**
850	58.28	7 *C*, ond *O* / witodlice
	51.17	**viro** *M*
851	58.29	hwæthugu *C*, hwæthwega *O* / sum þing
	51.18	**aliquid**
852	58.29	sænde *C*, sende *O* / asende
	51.18	**misisset**
853	58.29	geond / on
	51.18	**in**
854	58.30	ealle *C*, eall *O* / ælc
	51.18	**omnibus**
855	58.30	cigde / clypode
	51.18	**vocato**
856	58.31	sona / hrædlice
	51.18	**protinus**
857	59.3	cniht / cnapan
	51.21	**puerum**
858	59.4	wintreddan / treddan
	51.21	**calcaturio** *M*
859	59.7	gecyrde (gecirde *O*) eft / gehwearf
	51.24	**redit; redigit** V_2
860	59.9	gedon / geendodum
	51.25	**facta**
861	59.10	cigde / clypode
	51.25	**vocavit**
862	59.11	untynde *C*, ontynde *O* / geopenode
	51.25	**aperuit**
863	59.14	geat *C*, get *O* / ageat
	52.1	**fuderat; infuderat** *Maurists*
864	59.18	gyt *C*, git *O* / a
	52.2	**adhuc**
865	59.19	7 *C*, ond *O* / hwæt
866	59.20	arwyrða (arwurða *O*) wer / bisceop
867	59.21	ondrysenlice *C*, ondryslice *O* / egeslice
	52.3	**terribiliter**
868	59.24	næfre ænigum (ænegum *O*) / nanum
	52.4	**cuilibet; cuiquam** *Maurists*
869	59.26	atyddrian / aidlode
	52.6	**inaniscerit** *M*; **intumesceret** *Cl*
870	59.28	wære / wurde
871	59.29	gecnyssed *C*, gecnysed *O* / gebreged
	52.6	**pulsatus**

841 Both versions render *puerolo* twice, at 58.14 and 58.15. 849 *H* abbreviates ꝥ.

872 59.29 herenesse / wyrðmynde
52.5 **favore**
873 59.30 fram *C*, from *O* / on
52.5 **in**
874 59.30 þyssere *C*, ðisse *O* / þæs
875 59.31 wyrde / weorces
52.5 **facti**
876 59.32 lareowas (larewes *O*) ... Crist / hælendes
52.7 **magistri**
877 59.33 getrymede / getyde
52.8 **instrueret; introduceret** V_1, **duceret** *Maurists*, *var.*
878 59.35 þegnum / gingrum
52.8 **discipulis**
879 60.3 fram *C*, from *O* / of
52.10 **a**
880 60.4 genoh gecoplicu / gecwemlice
52.11 **apta; aperta** *Hf*
881 60.7 la / nu
882 60.10 bebead / het
52.13 **iussit**
883 60.12 gemærsodon *C*, gemærsedon *O* / gewidmærodon
52.13 **diffamaverunt** *C*
884 60.14 acenneda / ankenneda
52.14 **unigenitus**
885 60.16 wisan / þinge
52.15 **re**
886 60.19 hit *C*, *om.* *O* / þæt
52.16 **quod**
887 60.19 nanra (nane *O*) þinga / na
52.17 **menime** *M*
888 60.25 bysene / gebysnunge
52.19 **exemplo**
889 60.26 swaðe / fotswaðe
52.20 **vestigia**
890 60.28 unforspurnedum *C*, unforspornenen *O* / unætspornenum
52.20 **inoffenso**
891 61.1 bysene / gebysnunga
52.23 **exempla**
892 61.4 syn *C*, sin *O* / beon
893 61.5 nytte syn (sin *O*) / fremian
52.24 **prosint**
894 61.6 fulloft *C*, fuloft *O* / foroft
895 61.7 þæt / hit
896 61.7 byð *C*, bið *O* / si
52.25 **sit**
897 61.8 wilniað / gewilniað
53.1 **appetunt**
898 61.9 syn *C*, sin *O* / beon
899 61.9 [byð *C*, bið *O*] / si
53.1 **sit**
900 61.10 eadmodnesse *C*, eaðmoðnesse *O* / nyttlicnysse
53.1 **utilitatis; humilitatis** V_3, **aedificationis** W_2
901 61.11 nis hit / eornostlice
53.2 **ergo**
902 61.13 aht *C*, oht *O* / æni þing
53.3 **quicquam**
903 61.13 beon / gewurde
53.3 **fieri**
904 61.16 wilnian *C*, willan *O* / gewilnian
53.3 **velle**
905 61.17 wæron / gewurðan
53.4 **fiat**
906 61.21 ⁊swarode / to cwæð
907 61.22 hwylcehugu *C*, hwylchwega *O* / sume feawa
53.7 **pauca aliqua**
908 61.22 wisan / þinga
909 61.23 þa / þe
53.7 **quae**
910 61.25 þæs / his
53.8 **eius**
911 61.26 tid / timan
53.9 **tempore**
912 61.29 swyþe *C*, swiðe *O* / sum
913 61.33 þa þa / þonne
53.12 **cum**
914 62.7 ⁊ (ond *O*) þa / witodlice
53.15 **igitur**
915 62.8 com / becom
53.16 **venissit** *M*
916 62.9 beode *C*, *def.* *O* / mysan
53.16 **mensam**

888 Hecht could not decide between *bysne* and *bysene* for *O*. 899 Both the Latin and the revision repeat the form of 'to be' at 61.7 and 61.9; the original translation does not.

917 62.11 lofsang *C*, lofsong *O* / beodfers
53.17 **hymnum**
918 62.11 asægde / sunge
53.17 **diceret**
919 62.13 hergendlicum (heriendelice *O*) cræfte / gligcræfte
53.17 **ludendi arte**
920 62.14 semninga *C*, samninga *O* / færinga
53.18 **repente**
921 62.16 sona / hwæt
922 62.17 forhycgende *C*, forhicgende *O* / gehyrende
53.19 **dedignatus; audiens ... dedignatus** V_3
923 62.18 glig / sweg
53.19 **sonitum**
924 62.19 wa / wala
53.20 **heu**
925 62.22 herenysse *C*, herenesse *O* / lofe
53.21 **laudem; laudandum** *Maurists, var.*
926 62.22 ontynde / geopenode
53.21 **aperui**
927 62.25 þus / swaþeah
53.23 **ad-** *M*
928 62.26 godes / soðre
929 62.27 hwæþre / swaþeah
53.24 **tamen**
930 62.28 byð *C*, bið *O* / is
53.24 **est**
931 62.28 þa ... sona swa / ða þa
53.24 **dum**
932 62.30 onfeng / underfeng
54.1 **percepisset; accepisset** Pa_1
933 62.31 þurh / ut on
54.1 **e-** *C*
934 62.32 unmæte / ormæte
54.2 **ingens**
935 62.33 færinga / færlice
54.2 **subito**
936 62.34 ufan on / onufan
54.2 **in**
937 62.34 sloh / becom
54.3 **venit**
938 62.34 for / mid
54.3 **ex**
939 62.35 feoll *C*, gefeol *O* / astreht
54.3 **-stratus**
940 62.35 adune *C*, ofdune *O* / nyðer
54.3 **pro-**
941 63.1 upp *C*, up *O* / þanon
942 63.3 eallinga / eallunga
54.4 **funditus**
943 63.4 wisan / þinge
54.5 **re**
944 63.5 gehycganne *C*, gehicgane *O* / geþenceanne
54.5 **pensandum**
945 63.6 witan / hæbbenne
54.6 **exhibendus**
946 63.7 þa / hi
947 63.9 for / mid
948 63.11 eorre *C*, yrre *O* / yrsunge
54.7 **irascendum**
949 63.13 forþon / eornostlice
54.8 **ergo**
950 63.14 ma / swyðor
54.8 **tanto**
951 63.15 ma / swa
54.9 **quanto**
952 63.15 cuð / soð
54.9 **constat**
953 63.16 byð *C*, bið *O* / is
54.10 **est**
954 63.17 naht *C*, noht *O* / na
54.11 **non**
955 63.18 donne / on ... gebringenne
54.10 **inferendam; ferendam** V_3
956 63.22 sumre *C*, sume *O* / oðrum
54.12 **alio**
957 63.22 tide *C*, tid *O* / timan
54.12 **tempore**
958 63.25 bebohte / gesealde
54.13 **vindedit**
959 63.25 to / wið
960 63.28 sumdæl oðres *C*, hwæderhwæga oþer *O* / sum
54.14 **aliquod**
961 63.29 semninga *C*, sæmninga *O* / færinga
54.15 **subito**

919 Hecht reported *heriendlice* for *O*. **949** Hecht reported *forþo[ ]* for *O*. **960** Hecht reported *ge[ ]er*

No.	Ref.	Entry
962	63.31	biscope ***C***, bisceope ***O*** / bisceopstole
	54.15	**episcopum**
963	63.33	hwæthugu ***C***, hwæthwega ***O*** / sum þing
	54.17	**aliquid**
964	63.34	wædle / wædlunge
	54.17	**inopiae**
965	64.1	nyste / næfde
	54.18	**non habebat**
966	64.2	hatian ***C***, hatigean ***O*** / þefian
	54.18	**aestuare; stuari** ***St***$_1$
967	64.4	æmtige / idelhende
	54.19	**vacui**
968	64.5	semninga ***C***, sæmninga ***O*** / færinga
	54.19	**repente**
969	64.7	bebohte / gesealde
	54.21	**vindedissit** ***M***
970	64.8	þæt / þe
	54.20	**quem**
971†	64.12	eode ***C***, geeode ***O*** / stop
	54.22	**accessit**
972†	64.13	arfullice / arfæstlice
	54.23	**pie**
973†	64.13	nyd nimende ***C***, neod nymende ***O*** / stræc
	54.23	**violentus; violenter** ***Cl*****, validus** ***as a gloss La***
974†	64.14	tosloh / tobræc
	54.23	**comminuit**
975†	64.16	þa / hi
	54.24	**eos-**
976	64.18	⁊ ***C***, ond ***O*** / witodlice
	54.24	**itaque**
977	64.21	þæt / þe
	54.26	**quod**
978	64.26	buton (butan ***O***) tweon / untwylice
	55.3	**nimirum**
979	64.28	stefnum / hreame
	55.3	**voces**
980	64.29	com ***C***, cwom ***O*** / becom
	55.3	**advenit; venit** ***V***$_2$
981	64.30	biscopscire ***C***, bisceopscire ***O*** / bisceopwican
	55.3	**episcopio**
982	64.34	symble / þa
983	64.34	gecide / ceaste
	55.5	**iurgio**
984	65.4	wæs / wearð
985	65.6	in / into
	55.8	**in-**
986	65.9	sceate / reafe
	55.9	**vestimento**
987	65.11	þæt / mid hwam
	55.10	**unde**
988	65.12	preostes / mæssepreostas
	55.10	**praesbiteri**
989	65.12	unstilnysse ***C***, unstilnesse ***O*** / woffunga
	55.10	**insaniam**
990	65.14	sceat / grædan
	55.11	**vestimentum**
991	65.16	sceate / greadan
	55.12	**sinu**
992	65.17	lixende ***C***, lixiende ***O*** / scinende
	55.13	**fulgentes**
993	65.18	swa (***def. O***) swa / swilce
	55.13	**tamquam si**
994	65.20	gangende ***C***, gongende ***O*** / stop
	55.15	**-gressus**
995	65.23	sceate ***C***, sceat ***O*** / greadan
	55.15	**sinu**
996	65.24	loca / efne
	55.16	**ecce**
997	65.30	feoh / mancasas
	55.19	**solidos**
998	66.4	eac ***C***, eft ***O*** / soðlice
	55.22	**idem; quoque** ***Bo*****, namque** ***Cl*****, idem quoque** ***Pa***$_1$**, quidem** ***Pa***$_2$
999	66.4	sume / oðrum
	55.22	**alio**

hwu(u?)g[ ]oþer for *O;* Johnson, *ge[ ]der hwugu oþer,* with the two *u*'s uncertain (Transcript, p. 48); and Harting, *gehwæðer hwaga oþer* (p. 281, n. 2). Read *ge[ ]hwæderhwæga oþer,* beside *C*'s *gewat feran ut sumdæl oðres* and *H*'s *ut gewat sum.* **970** *C* and *O* abbreviate *ꝥ.* **977** *C* and *O* abbreviate *ꝥ.* **980** Hecht reported *[ ]wom* for *O.* **981** Hecht reported *bisceoprican* for *H,* though the wynn is unmistakable. **994** Hecht printed *utgangende* for *C,* beside *H*'s *stop ut. O* has *[ ]gongende.* **998** Hecht's critical apparatus leaves it unclear whether he reported *eac hit eft* or *hit eft* for *O.* In fact, the manuscript reads *eft hit,* beside *C*'s *eac hit.*

1000 66.4 tid / timan
55.22 **tempore**
1001 66.12 underngeweorce / gereorde
56.2 **prandio**
1002 66.14 7 / þa
56.4 **autem**
1003 66.15 gewunodon *C*, gewunedon *O* / wunodon
56.4 **morati**
1004 66.16 fram *C*, from *O* / æt
56.5 **a**
1005 66.17 daga gehwylce / dæghwamlice
56.5 **cottidie**
1006 66.21 comon *C*, [ ]comon *O* / becomon
56.6 **-versi**
1007 66.22 geblunnon *C*, blunnon *O* / geswicon
56.7 **cessarent**
1008 66.24 nanes *C*, no *O* / næfre
56.8 **numquam**
1009 66.25 swa / swaþeah
56.7 **tamen**
1010 66.26 ongitanne *C*, ongytanne *O* / akenned
1011 66.26 swa swa / swilce
56.8 **ac si**
1012 66.32 com / becom
56.10 **-venit**
1013 67.2 wisan / þing
56.11 **ea**
1014 67.2 sæde *C*, sægde *O* / rehte
56.11 **narrat**
1015 67.3 swigunge / swigan
56.11 **silentio**
1016 67.5 in / into
56.12 **in-**
1017 67.7 unasecgendlicu *C*, unasægcendlicre *O* / micelre
56.12 **magna**
1018 67.10 gecyrde *C*, oncirde *O* / bewende
56.14 **conversus**
1019 67.17 *om. C*, þanon *O* / endemes
1020 67.17 gangende *C*, gongende *O* / ferdon
56.17 **-gressae**
1021 67.18 anlipig *C*, ænlipe *O* / furðon
56.17 **quidem**
1022 67.19 fæce ... wearðes (wurtgeardes *O*) / wyrttunhege
56.17 **spatium horti**
1023 67.19 to lafe (...) wunode (wurde *O*) / belaf
56.18 **remanerit** ***M***
1024 67.25 wisan / þing
56.18 **haec**
1025 67.25 secgaþ *C*, secgen *O* / cyðon
56.19 **narramus**
1026 67.25 tide / timan
56.19 **tempore**
1027 67.26 nu / þa þa
56.19 **quando**
1028 67.27 þa geo *C*, geara iu *O* / eallunga
56.19 **iam**
1029 67.29 ge eac swylce / 7
56.20 **et**
1030 67.30 7 / þonne
56.20 **dum**
1031 67.32 cyþde / sæde
56.22 **testatur**
1032 68.3 cwæð / sæde
56.22 **ait**
1033 68.3 tid / timan
56.22 **tempore**
1034 68.5 gangende *C*, gongende *O* / agan
56.23 **-gressus**
1035 68.6 fulloft *C*, fuloft *O* / foroft
56.23 **nonnumquam**
1036 68.8 on (to *O*) ... huse / ham
56.24 **re-**
1037 68.8 cyrde *C*, cirde *O* / gecyrde
56.24 **-vertebatur**
1038 68.11 ungyrdende *C*, ongyrwendne *O* / bereafode
56.25 **expolians; spolians** ***La***
1039 68.12 gescrydde *C*, gesrydde *O* / scrydde
56.25 **vestiebat**
1040 68.14 geearnode / gescrydde
57.1 **vestirit** ***M***

1020 Hecht printed *utgangende* and *utferdon*. **1031** Hecht reported *cyþðe* for *CO*. **1034** Hecht printed *utgangende* for *C*, *ut agan* for *H*, beside *O*'s *ut ... gongende*.

1041 68.17 mid wordum (wordom *O*) þreade / cidde
57.2 **increpare**
1042 68.19 þearfendum mannum (monnum *O*) / þearfum
57.3 **pauperibus**
1043 68.22 gemette / afunde
57.5 **invenit**
1044 68.23 neah *C*, fulneah *O* / forneah
57.4 **paene**
1045 68.25 þearfendum mannum *C*, in ðearfena ælmessan *O* / þearfum
57.5 **pauperibus**
1046 68.26 *om. C*, g[ ]g[ ] *O* / begiten
57.5 **paraverat**
1047 68.27 þerscan *C*, ðerscean *O* / beatan
57.6 **tunderit** *M*
1048 68.28 ge / 7
57.6 **-que**
1049 68.30 to lore gedon / forspilled
57.7 **perdedissit** *M*
1050 68.31 bigleofa *C*, ondlyfen *O* / help
57.6 **subsidia**
1051 68.31 com *C*, cwom *O* / becom
57.7 **-venit**
1052 69.2 onfon / undernam
57.9 **admitterit** *M*
1053 69.4 gan / gangan
57.9 **-ire**
1054 69.12 gefylled / full
57.13 **plenum**
1055 69.13 gefægnode *C*, gefeah *O* / geblissode
57.14 **gaudebat**
1056 69.14 *om. C*, gesamnod *O* / gegaderod
57.14 **congregasse; congressae** V_4
1057 69.16 wæs / wearð
1058 69.18 secgan / biddan
57.15 **agere; rogare** *as a gloss Sa*, **cogere** *Maurists, var.*
1059 69.18 forþon (forðan *O*) þe / þæt
57.16 **ut**
1060 69.19 swylce / swa ... swa
1061 69.19 forgæf *C*, forgeaf *O* / sealde
57.16 **daret**
1062 69.19 he / se
57.16 **qui**
1063 69.20 swa hwæt swa / þa þing þe
57.16 **quae**
1064 69.24 eac / witodlice
57.17 **itaque**
1065 69.26 ingange *C*, ingonge *O* / cafortune
57.17 **vestibulo**
1066 69.27 þa / hig
57.18 **eas**
1067 69.27 afyrrde 7 bereafode *C*, afirde 7 ongereafode *O* / aweg bær 7 abat
57.18 **auferebat**
1068 69.28 geneahhe *C*, geneahche *O* / gelomlice
1069 69.28 naht feorran *C*, noht feo[ ]ran *O* / of ... neahlande
57.18 **ex vicinitate (vicino rure *C*, vicino *S*)**
1070 69.29 þa / soðlice
57.19 **viro** *M*
1071 70.1 ingange *C*, i[ ]gonge *O* / cafortune
57.19 **vestibulo**
1072 70.2 þeaw / gewuna
57.20 **more**
1073 70.2 genam *C*, genom *O* / gelæhte
57.20 **abstulit; exstulit** *changed to* **abstulit** W_2
1074 70.3 gearn *C*, georn *O* / arn
57.21 **-travit**
1075 70.3 to / into
57.21 **in-**
1076 70.6 min / leofa
1077 70.8 geseoh / 7 efne
57.23 **ecce enim**
1078 70.9 se / þes
1079 70.10 fedde / afedde
57.23 **nutrit**
1080 70.17 geæadmodað *C*, geeaðmodað *O* / gemedemode

1046 When undamaged, *O* probably read *gegearwod;* cf. 19.33 *gegearwian* C, *gegearwigean* O / *begitan.* Hecht reported the manuscript as defective, but Johnson made out the first *g* and suggested the reading *gegearwode* (Transcript, p. 51). **1059** *H* abbreviates ꝥ. **1063** Clark Hall-Meritt enters the compound *swahwætswa,* yet under *swa* it lists *swa hwa swa, swa hwilc swa,* and other phrases.

58.2 **dignatur**
1081 70.19 yfellicum *C*, yfe[ ]cum *O* / wacum
58.2 **vilibus**
1082 70.20 wisum / þingum
58.2 **rebus**
1083 70.26 yfellicum / waclicum
58.5 **vilibus**
1084 70.32 cwiðst *C*, cwist *O* / sægst
58.8 **dicis**
1085 70.34 7swarode / to cwæð
1086 70.35 swiþe / eac
58.9 **quoque**
1087 71.1 wæs nama (noma *O*) / genemned
58.10 **nomine**
1088 71.4 unmætre *C*, unmættre *O* / ormætes
58.11 **inmensae; inmundis inmensae** ***Bo*****, immundis** ***Hf*****, malignis** ***Maurists*****,** ***var.***
1089 71.8 fuloft / foroft
58.12 **nonnumquam**
1090 71.8 weoredu *C*, weorudu *O* / eoredweredu
58.13 **legiones**
1091 71.9 adraf / adræfde
58.13 **pellerit** ***M*****; expelleret** ***Pa_2***
1092 71.10 geswencton / asettum
58.12 **obsessis**
1093 71.10 geornfull *C*, geornful *O* / atiht
58.13 **intentus; ofpositus** ***as a gloss La***
1094 71.11 teolone *C*, tolene *O* / bigenge
58.13 **studio**
1095 71.11 singalra *C*, sin[ ]alra *O* / singallice
58.13 **continuae**
1096 71.12 þem *C*, þam *O* / him
58.14 **se**
1097 71.12 gesettum / standendan
58.14 **obiectas; subiectas** ***M***
1098 71.18 he / se
58.16 **qui**
1099 71.18 wæs / wearð
58.16 **est**
1100 71.18 unfyrn / for lyttlum fyrste
58.16 **non longum tempus**
1101 71.19 for / of
1102 71.20 gesægenum *C*, gesegenum *O* / sægene
58.17 **relatione**
1103 71.24 bylde *C*, byldo *O* / gedyrstlæcinge
58.18 **ausu**
1104 71.24 æfter þon / syððon
58.18 **post**
1105 71.26 trymnysse *C*, trymnesse *O* / trymminge
59.1 **instructionem**
1106 71.27 swa ... swa / swilce
59.1 **quasi**
1107 71.30 in ... neahdælum / neah ... dælum
59.2 **in vicinis**
1108 71.33 wæs / wearð
59.5 **fuerat**
1109 72.3 þa / soðlice
59.5 **viro**
1110 72.6 sprecenan / cwedenan
59.6 **-dicti**
1111 72.12 ingeþohte *C*, ingeþonce *O* / geþohte
59.8 **conscientiam**
1112 72.16 forðgang *C*, forðgong *O* / fare
59.9 **processionem**
1113 72.18 ma / swyðor
59.10 **plus**
1114 72.24 þær / þyder
1115 72.30 cyrcan *C*, ciricean *O* / gebedhuses
59.14 **oratorii**
1116 72.32 sona / þa hrædlice
59.16 **protinus**
1117 73.1 7 *C*, ond *O* / ac
59.16 **sed**
1118 73.1 þa / eac
59.17 **simul**
1119 73.1 sona / færinga
59.17 **repente**
1120 73.1 eode *C*, geeode *O* / gefor
59.17 **-vasit**
1121 73.3 mægn *C*, magan *O* / mihta
59.17 **vires**

1110 Hecht printed *foresprecenan* and *forecwedenan*.

1122 73.3 aht swylces *C*, oht sw[ ]ces *O* / æni þing
59.17 **quicquam**

1123 73.4 geneþan / gedyrstlæcean
59.18 **praesumere**

1124 73.4 wæs / wearð
59.18 **est**

1125 73.4 genyded / geneadod
59.18 **conpulsus**

1126 73.6 ongytan *C*, ongitan *O* / oncneowe
59.18 **cognuscere** *M*

1127 73.8 namon / genamon
59.20 **sublatam**

1128 73.8 on / of
59.19 **ex**

1129 73.9 mid ... handum (hondum *O*) / handlunga
59.19 **in manibus**

1130 73.11 langre *C*, longre *O* / singalre
59.21 **continua**

1131 73.12 bregde / gedrehte
59.21 **adtererit** *M*

1132 73.12 þis / þæt
59.21 **hanc**

1133 73.13 swyðe *C*, swiðe *O* / þearle
59.21 **vehementer**

1134 73.14 for / on

1135 73.14 lufan / lufunge
59.22 **amando**

1136 73.15 mid / ehtende
59.22 **persequentis**

1137 73.17 to þon / swa

1138 73.19 scrifan *C*, scrifon *O* / hogodon

1139 73.19 eallinga *C*, [ ]lenga *O* / eallunga
59.24 **funditus; a radice fundit** *as a gloss La*

1140 73.20 ongunnon / woldon
59.25 **conaretur**

1141 73.21 hi / þa

1142 73.21 helpan / gehelpan
59.25 **prodesse**

1143 73.23 wæs / wearð
59.25 **est**

1144 73.23 anre / sumre

1145 73.24 bedypped / bedyfed
60.1 **mersa; missa** *as a gloss La*

1146 73.25 ongunnon / syrwdon
60.2 **moliebantur; parabantur** *as a gloss La*

1147 73.26 langum *C*, longum *O* / langsumum
60.1 **diutinis; diuturnis** *M*, **diutius** *as a gloss La*, **diu** St_1

1148 73.26 onsangum *C*, onsongum *O* / galdrum
60.1 **incantationibus**

1149 73.27 oðþæt / þæt
60.2 **ut**

1150 73.29 for / mid

1151 73.31 wæs / wearð

1152 73.32 forcyrdan *C*, forcerdan *O* / forhwyrfedum
60.3 **perversa**

1153 73.33 sona / færinga
60.4 **subito**

1154 73.33 mæniu *C*, mænigu *O* / eoredmeniu
60.4 **legio**

1155 74.1 on / of
60.5 **ex**

1156 74.2 manegum *C*, monigum *O* / fela
60.5 **tot**

1157 74.2 styrenyssum / styrungum
60.5 **motibus**

1158 74.3 manegum *C*, monegum *O* / fela
60.5 **tot**

1159 74.4 cleopungum *C*, clypencgum *O* / hreamum
60.5 **clamoribus-**

1160 74.5 efne / swa
60.6 **quot**

1161 74.5 fram *C*, from *O* / mid

1162 74.5 manegum *C*, monegum *O* / fela
60.6 **[quot]**

1163 74.7 eodon (geeodon *O*) ... in geþeaht / ongunnon ... þeahtian
60.6 **inito consilio**

1164 74.8 geandetton *C*, geondetton *O* / andetton
60.7 **fatentes; patentes** *as a gloss La*

1140 The rubricator of *O* supplied the last three letters, *non*.

1162 Both *efne swa ... manegum* and *swa fela swa* render *quot*.

1165	74.9	ungeleafan / ungeleaffulnysse
	60.7	**perfidiae**
1166	74.9	scyld / gylt
	60.7	**culpam**
1167	74.14	to / mid
1168	74.14	onfeng / underfeng
	60.9	**suscepta**
1169	74.17	ma / swiðor
	60.10	**tanto-**
1170	74.17	gefealh / befealh
	60.10	**incubuit; iniunxit** *as a gloss La*
1171	74.18	geornnysse *C*, geornesse *O* / geornfullnysse
	60.10	**adnisu; conamine** *as a gloss La*, **innisu** Pa_1
1172	74.19	ma / swa
	60.10	**quanto**
1173	74.21	weorod *C*, werod *O* / ormætan truman
	60.11	**aciem; pugnam** *as a gloss La*
1174	74.21	mænigeo *C*, mænigo *O* / eoredmenigeo
	60.11	**legionis**
1175	74.22	ymb *C*, embe *O* / æfter
	60.11	**post**
1176	74.22	manega *C*, unmanega *O* / feawum
	60.11	**non ... multos**
1177	74.25	ænigne / nænne
	60.13	**proprium**
1178	74.29	tid / timan
	60.14	**tempore**
1179	74.31	adraf / adræfde
	60.15	**excussit**
1180	75.4	dyglu *C*, digle *O* / stille
	60.16	**secretam**
1181	75.4	geonlicte *C*, geonlihte *O* / gehiwode
	60.17	**simulans**
1182	75.6	gan / faran
	60.18	**-ire**
1183	75.7	cwæð *C*, cweðan *O* / clypian
	60.18	**clamare**
1184	75.7	nu / la
	60.18	**o**
1185	75.12	nu / ⁊
	60.21	**et**
1186	75.18	laðode / in gelaðode
	60.23	**invitavit**
1187	75.20	dyde / gedyde
	60.24	**fecit**
1188	75.21	betwux *C*, betwih *O* / betweonon
	60.24	**vicissim**
1189	75.22	ætnexstan *C*, ætnehstan *O* / þa
1190	75.28	ongæt *C*, ongeat *O* / oncneow
	61.3	**agnovit**
1191	75.29	feormode / underfeng
	61.2	**susceperit**
1192	75.29	ge eac / oððe
	61.3	**vel**
1193	75.30	adraf / adræfde
	61.3	**-pulissit** *M*
1194	75.33	bylde *C*, byldo *O* / dyrstinysse
	61.4	**ausum**
1195	76.6	soðfæstnys *C*, soðfæstnes *O* / hælend
	61.8	**veritas; dominus** Pa_1
1196	76.10	þonne / gif
	61.10	**cum**
1197	76.11	woh ⁊ forcyrred (forcerred *O*) / forhwyrfed
	61.10	**perversa**
1198	76.12	gangeþ / stæpð
	61.11	**-cedit**
1199	76.14	forþon / soðlice
	61.12	**namque**
1200	76.15	mid / on
1201	76.16	mode / weorke
	61.13	**opere**
1202	76.16	mid *C*, him *O* / on
1203	76.17	tælnysse *C*, tælnesse *O* / tælinge
	61.14	**derogatione; detectione** *as a gloss La*
1204	76.18	wæs / wearð
	61.13	**est**
1205	76.18	se / he
	61.12	**qui**
1206	76.19	gestliþnysse *C*, gestliðnesse *O* / cumliðnysse
	61.12	**hospitalitatem; hospitalem** *Bo*
1207	76.20	soðlice / ac

1198 Hecht printed *foregangeþ* and *forestæpð*. **1202** Hecht reported *mid* for *O*.

61.14 **nam**
1208 76.21 cyþde *C, def. O* / gecyðde
61.15 **innotuit**
1209 76.22 ærre / forestæppende
61.15 **praecedens**
1210 76.22 feormung / underfangennys
61.15 **susceptio**
1211 76.23 eac swylce / witodlice
61.16 **namque**
1212 76.24 manige *C*, monige *O* / fela
61.16 **nonnulli**
1213 76.25 tiliað *C*, [ ]liað *O* / þenceað
61.16 **student**
1214 76.25 don / wyrceanne
61.16 **facere**
1215 76.25 þe / þæt
61.16 **ut**
1216 76.26 gedwellan *C*, dwellan *O* / adilgian
61.17 **obnubilent; obtegerunt** *as a gloss La*
1217 76.27 na *C*, no *O* / ne
61.17 **nec**
1218 76.28 þæt / þe
1219 76.28 mycclum *C*, miclum *O* / aht swiðe
1220 76.30 ma / swyðor
1221 76.30 wyllað / gewilniað
1222 76.31 syn *C*, sin *O* / beon
1223 76.31 beforan / toforan
61.18 **qua**
1224 76.32 for / be
61.18 **de**
1225 76.32 wisan *C*, wi[ ]an *O* / þinge
61.18 **re**
1226 77.1 ma / swyðor
61.20 **potius**
1227 77.1 behealdan / begyman
61.20 **intendisse**
1228 77.3 gestliþnysse *C*, gestliðnesse *O* / cumliðnysse
61.19 **hospitalitate**
1229 77.3 onfeng / underfeng
61.19 **suscepit**
1230 77.3 æteownysse *C*, æteawnesse *O* / bounge
61.20 **ostentatione**
1231 77.6 betran / arfæstum
1232 77.6 dæde / weorke
61.20 **operi**
1233 77.8 gesewen / geþuht
61.21 **videretur**
1234 77.9 þæt / swylce
61.20 **ut**
1235 77.9 lifes wære / dyde
61.21 **fecisse**
1236 77.10 onfeng / underfeng
61.21 **susceperit**
1237 77.12 onweg / ut
61.22 **ex-**
1238 77.18 ⁊swarode / cwæð
1239 77.19 sægð *C*, swylce *O* / gelamp
1240 77.21 wæs / wearð
1241 77.21 godes / halgan
1242 77.22 gewilnode *C*, gewilnade *O* / begeat
62.3 **impetravit; imperavit** *M*
1243 77.25 godes / drihtnes
62.3 **dei; domini** *CI*
1244 77.25 gedon ⁊ gefylled / geendod
62.3 **facta**
1245 77.27 ofer / on
62.4 **in-**
1246 77.28 bysenan *C*, bysnan *O* / blindan
1247 77.28 þa sona / þærrihte
62.4 **protinus**
1248 77.31 ⁊ ufan þæt eac *C*, onufan þæt eac *O* / eft syððon
62.5 **praeterea**
1249 77.32 militisces mannes (monnes *O*) / þegenes
62.5 **militis**
1250 77.33 wæs / wearð
62.6 **fuerat**
1251 77.33 gecyrred *C*, gecirred *O* / awend
62.6 **versus**
1252 77.33 myccle *C*, micle *O* / feondlice
1253 78.1 uneaþe / earfoðlice

1208 Hecht reported *cyþðe* for *C*. 1210 *O* actually has eight minims between *r* and *g*. 1213 Hecht reported *[ ]ð* for *O*. 1215 *H* abbreviates *ꝥ*. 1218 *C* and *O* abbreviate *ꝥ*. 1225 Hecht reported *wi[ ]* for *O*. 1246 Hecht reported *bysenan* for *O*.

62.6 **vix**

1254 78.3 *om. C*, ongefaran *O* / ongeræsan
62.7 **invadere**

1255 78.4 wundode ... mid bitu (bitum *O*)/ bat 7 ... totær
62.7 **morsibus delaniarit (laniaret *changed to* dilaniaret *La*)**

1256 78.5 þeh *C*, hwæthwega *O* / ætnextan
62.8 **utcumque; namque Pa_1**

1257 78.7 wæs / wearð
62.9 **est**

1258 78.11 gecyrde *C*, gecirde *O* / awende
62.10 **mutavit**

1259 78.12 manþwærnysse *C*, manþwæ[ ]nesse *O* / geþwærnysse
62.10 **mansuitudinem**

1260 78.13 *om. C*, æfter þon *O* / syððon
62.11 **post; postea *C***

1261 78.14 wedendra heortnysse *C*, wede[ ]heortnesse *O* / wodnysse
62.11 **vesaniam; insaniam *Maurists***

1262 78.16 acyrred *C*, acirred *O* / awended
62.13 **inmutatum**

1263 78.16 wedendra heorta *C*, wedenheortnesse *O* / wodnysse
62.13 **vesania; vexatione *Sa***

1264 78.19 bebead / geteohhode
62.14 **decrevit**

1265 78.20 eft bringan (brincgan *O*) / forgifenne
62.14 **offerendum**

1266 78.23 wilnunge *C*, wilnuncge *O* / benum
62.15 **praecibus**

1267 78.26 healfne / midne ... twegra dæla
62.16 **mediam duarum (utrarumque *Cl*) partium**

1268 78.26 geferde / healdende
62.16 **tenens**

1269 78.27 militiscan mannes *C*, militiscean monnes *O* / þegenes
62.17 **militis**

1270 78.27 gehyrde / getiðode
62.17 **audivit**

1271 78.28 7 / ge
62.17 **et**

1272 78.28 hwæþre / eac

1273 78.28 wiðsoc / forsoc
62.18 **recusavit**

1274 78.29 habban *C*, healdan *O* / underfonne
62.17 **suscepere; recipere *Maurists***

1275 78.30 gebedenum / begitenum
62.17 **exhibita; -hibita V_3**

1276 78.32 æfter þan (þon *O*) / syððan
62.18 **post; postea Pa_1**

1277 78.32 nam *C*, nom *O* / underfeng
62.19 **suscepit; accepit *C***

1278 79.5 nydendre *C*, neðendre *O* / neadiendre
62.20 **cogente**

1279 79.6 þearf / neod
62.21 **necessarium**

1280 79.10 þis / þæt
62.22 **hoc**

1281 79.11 ongæt *C*, ong[ ] *O* / oncneow
62.23 **agnovi**

1282 79.11 anum ... huhugu (hwæthwega *O*) swa / nealice
62.23 **fere**

1283 79.12 nihtum / dagum
62.23 **dies**

1284 79.12 þa / witodlice
62.23 **namque; autem V_3**

1285 79.15 hwæt / hwanone
63.2 **unde**

1286 79.21 frine *C*, frigne *O* / axie
63.4 **quaeso**

1287 79.25 ongæte *C*, ongeate *O* / oncneowe
63.6 **cognovisti; nosti *M***

1288 79.32 efne / sona
63.9 **ita**

1289 79.33 swa / þærrihte
63.9 **[ita]**

1290 79.33 wæs tyðe *C*, abæd *O* / beget
63.9 **impetravit; imperavit *M***

1263 Hecht gave *insania* for the Latin (*Einleitung*, p. 150), but his only acknowledged source, the Maurists' printed edition, has *vesania*. Cf. entry **1261.** **1278** Hecht reported *nedendre* for *O*. **1289** Both *efne* and *swa*, or *sona* and *þærrihte*, may help render *ita*.

1291	80.6	⁊ *C*, ond *O* / þa
	63.12	**sed; et *Maurists***
1292	80.7	æhte / lande
	63.13	**possessione**
1293	80.8	cnihtas / cnapan
	63.12	**puerolos**
1294	80.8	æht / land
	63.13	**possessio**
1295	80.10	midþy þe *C*, midþi *O* / þa þa
	63.14	**cum**
1296	80.10	wæs / wearð
	63.15	**fuisset**
1297	80.11	gebodod *C*, bodad *O* / gecyðed
	63.15	**nuntiatum**
1298	80.13	gecigan *C*, gecigean *O* / gelangian
	63.16	**vocari; evocari V_2**
1299	80.16	wordum / spræce
	63.16	**sermone**
1300	80.16	tihhode *C*, tihhade *O* / þohte
	63.17	**studuit**
1301	80.16	sceolde / wolde
1302	80.17	geliðian / gegladian
	63.17	**placare**
1303	80.18	æfter þon / syððon
	63.17	**post**
1304	80.21	cnihtas / cnapan
	63.18	**puerulos; pueros V_3**
1305	80.22	gegearwiað / getiðiað
	63.19	**praebete**
1306	80.22	þæt / þyses
	63.19	**hoc**
1307	80.24	yldost / fyrmest
	63.20	**prior**
1308	80.27	witodlice / gewisslice
	63.21	**nam**
1309	80.27	cnihtas / cnapan
	63.21	**pueros; puerulos *C***
1310	80.29	beotigende *C*, beotiende *O* / þywde
	63.22	**minatus**
1311	80.30	þam / hine
	63.22	**cui**
1312	80.31	hyran / gehyran
	63.23	**audis**
1313	80.33	unrotsian / geunrodsa
	63.24	**contristare**
1314	81.1	ofþynce *C*, ne helpe *O* / ne fremie
	63.24	**non expediat**
1315	81.4	onweg / þanon
	64.1	**dis-**
1316	81.5	eode / faran
	64.2	**digressurus**
1317	81.8	cwedena *C*, cwedenra *O* / sædra
	64.3	**-dictis**
1318	81.9	cnihta / cnapena
	64.3	**puerolis *M***
1319	81.10	geþafa beon / geþwærian
	64.4	**consentire**
1320	81.11	wæs / wearð
1321	81.13	helpeð / fremað
	64.5	**expedit**
1322	81.13	ga / gewite
	64.6	**-cedis**
1323	81.15	eft gecyrde (gecirde *O*) / gewennde
	64.7	**reversus**
1324	81.16	huse / inne
	64.7	**hospitium**
1325	81.16	cnihtas *C*, [ ]tas *O* / cnapan
	64.7	**pueros; puerulos Pa_2**
1326	81.17	on / uppon
	64.8	**super-**
1327	81.17	be *C*, bi *O* / ymbe
	64.7	**de**
1328	81.17	þam / þe
	64.7	**quibus**
1329	81.18	gedon / sprecað
	64.7	**agebatur**
1330	81.18	sænde *C*, sende *O* / asende
	64.8	**-misit**
1331	81.18	beforan *C*, [ ]foran *O* / forð
	64.8	**prae-**
1332	81.20	sona / þærrihte
	64.9	**statim**
1333	81.20	strad / astah
	64.9	**-scendens**
1334	81.21	farende / fyliende
	64.9	**-secutus *C***

1299 Hecht reported *worðum* for *CO*. 1317 Hecht printed *forecweden(r)a* and *foresædra*. 1334 Hecht printed *æfterfarende* and *æfterfyliende*.

1335 81.22 com *C*, cwom *O* / becom
64.10 **venissit** *M*
1336 81.26 gefeoll / afeoll
64.11 **-ruit**
1337 81.26 scanca *C*, sconca *O* / þeoh
64.12 **coxa**
1338 81.27 tobrocen / forbærst
64.12 **confracta; fracta** *La*
1339 81.28 wæs / wearð
64.12 **essit** *M*
1340 81.30 cumena huse / inne
64.13 **hospitium**
1341 81.31 sona / ofstlice
64.14 **festinus**
1342 81.31 sænde (sende *O*) ... ham / ofsennde 7 ongean gelædde
64.14 **misit et ... reduxit**
1343 81.31 cnihtas / cnapan
64.14 **pueros**
1344 81.32 beforan / forð
64.14 **prae-**
1345 81.32 sænde *C*, sende *O* / asende
64.14 **-miserat**
1346 81.32 bead / asende
64.15 **mandavit**
1347 82.2 sona swa / ða þa
64.16 **dum; cum** O_2
1348 82.3 cnihtas / cnapan
64.17 **pueros; puerolos** V_2
1349 82.4 toforan / tomiddes forð
64.18 **ad medium**
1350 82.5 forsoc / wiðsoc
64.17 **negaverat; denegaverat** *Bo*
1351 82.11 nime / hæbbe
64.20 **recipe**
1352 82.12 cnihtas / cnapan
64.20 **pueros**
1353 82.13 onfeng *C*, onfencg *O* / underfeng
64.21 **susceptus**
1354 82.13 cnihtas *C*, cnihtum *O* / cnapan
64.21 **puerolos** V_2; **pueros** *Hf*
1355 82.14 sona / þærrihte
64.23 **statim**
1356 82.17 stregd *C*, astregd *O* / spreng
64.24 **proice**
1357 82.19 soðlice / witodlice
64.24 **itaque**
1358 82.21 eode / stop
64.25 **-gressus**
1359 82.22 stregde *C*, stregd[ ] *O* / sprengde
64.26 **aspersit**
1360 82.23 wise / þing
64.26 **res**
1361 82.26 scancan *C*, sconcan *O* / þeoh
65.1 **coxam**
1362 82.28 sceancan *C*, sconcan *O* / þeo
65.2 **coxa**
1363 82.30 ræste / bedde
65.2 **lecto**
1364 82.31 eode / wearð
65.3 **-scenso**
1365 82.31 to / uppon
65.3 **a-**
1366 82.33 geþrowode *C*, geðrowade *O* / þolode
65.4 **pertulissit** *M*
1367 82.34 ænige *C*, æni[ ] *O* / nane
65.4 **nullam; ullam** *M*
1368 82.34 deringe *C*, [ ]eringe *O* / derunge
65.4 **lesionem** *C*
1369 83.5 cnihtas / cnapan
65.5 **pueros**
1370 83.5 for / wið
65.5 **cum**
1371 83.5 wæs / wearð
1372 83.6 genyded *C*, genided *O* / geneadod
65.7 **subactus; coactus** *C*, **invitus** *as a gloss La*
1373 83.7 ceape / weorðe
65.6 **praetio**
1374 83.9 gefylled / geendodum
65.7 **expletis**
1375 83.10 tihhode *C*, tihade *O* / geteohhode
65.7 **studebat**
1376 83.11 sæde *C*, sægde *O* / gerehte
65.8 **narrare**
1377 83.11 oðre / ma
65.8 **alia**
1378 83.11 wisan / þinga
1379 83.14 wæs / wearð

1340 Hecht printed *cumenahuse.*

1380 83.15 afeoll *C*, onfeoll *O* / asah
65.9 **incubuerat**
1381 83.21 þingum / bysgungum
1382 83.24 wisan / þing
65.12 **rem**
1383 83.24 sæde *C*, sægde *O* / cwæð
65.13 **dicens**
1384 83.30 he / se
65.15 **qui**
1385 83.30 ðæs / his
1386 83.31 mettrumnesse *C*, mettrumness *O* / untrumnysse
65.15 **molestia**
1387 83.31 wæs / wearð
65.16 **est**
1388 83.33 easterlican æfenne (æfene *O*) / easteræfenne
65.15 **vespere ... paschali**
1389 83.33 þæs / his
65.16 **cuius**
1390 84.3 hwylchugu *C*, hwylchwega *O* / sumre
1391 84.6 byrgene *C*, byrgenne *O* / bebyrginge
65.19 **sepulturae**
1392 84.7 wæron / wurdon
1393 84.9 halgan / arwurðan
65.20 **venerabilem**
1394 84.15 uncerne / urne
65.23 **nostrum**
1395 84.16 ongæt *C*, ongeat *O* / wiste
65.23 **cognovit; agnovit** *M*
1396 84.19 wifum / swystrum
1397 84.19 anweg *C*, onweg *O* / heonone
66.1 **re-**
1398 84.20 secge / spreke
66.1 **dicere**
1399 84.20 git / ge
1400 84.23 naht *C*, n[ ] *O* / nan man
66.2 **nullus hominum**
1401 84.24 onweg / þanone
66.3 **dis-**
1402 84.25 gewunode *C*, gewuno[ ] *O* / wunode
66.3 **mansit; remansit** *C*, **permansit** *C*/
1403 84.31 eode / genealæhte
66.5 **perrexit ... accessit**
1404 84.33 orsawla / sawulleasa
66.6 **exanimae**
1405 85.1 7 / soðlice
66.7 **autem**
1406 85.1 gefyldum / geendodre
66.7 **expleta**
1407 85.1 gebede / bene
66.7 **praece; orationem** *M*
1408 85.3 unlifigendan / deadan
66.8 **defuncti**
1409 85.4 gecigde *C*, cigde *O* / nemde 7 clypode
66.9 **vocavit; clamavit** *C*
1410 85.7 gelice þon / þa
66.9 **autem**
1411 85.8 wæs / wearð
66.10 **fuissit** *M*
1412 85.9 nealecan *C*, nealican *O* / nealæcendan
66.10 **vicinam**
1413 85.9 medmicclu *C*, medlicu *O* / gehwæde
66.10 **modicam**
1414 85.10 sona / þærrihte
66.11 **statim**
1415 85.10 untynde *C*, ontynde *O* / geopenode
66.11 **aperuit**
1416 85.14 þam / him
66.12 **cui**
1417 85.20 onsended / send
66.15 **missus**
1418 85.23 com *C*, cwom *O* / becom
66.16 **venit**
1419 85.23 on *C*, in *O* / into
66.16 **in**
1420 85.24 gecigde / clypode
1421 85.24 gefyldum / geendodum
66.17 **expletis**
1422 85.26 gelæded *C*, gehæled *O* / gestrangod
66.17 **convaluit**
1423 85.28 hwæþre / swaþeah

1390 *O*'s rubricator inserted the *c*. **1400** Hecht reported *O* as defective. **1402** Hecht reported *gewun[ ]* for *O*.

66.18 **tamen**

1424 85.31 ænig (nænig *O*) tweo / untwylice
66.19 **dubium non**

1425 85.34 symble *C*, simble *O* / eac
66.20 **et**

1426 85.34 tilode 7 wilnode (wilnade *O*) / hogode
66.21 **studuit**

1427 85.35 licode *C*, licade *O* / gelicienne
66.21 **placere**

1428 86.2 swa / þus

1429 86.2 todæge / þonne
66.22 **cum**

1430 86.4 manige *C*, monige *O* / fela
66.22 **tot**

1431 86.5 onlyseð *C*, on[ ] *O* / unbundene
66.23 **absolvere**

1432 86.7 of *C*, [ ]f *O* / mid
66.24 **ex**

1433 86.9 cwic / libbende
66.24 **vivens; vivos** St_1

1434 86.9 deþ / wyrcenne
66.25 **facere**

1435 86.10 unablinnendlice *C*, unablinnedlice *O* / ungeswikendlice
66.24 **indesinenter**

1436 86.10 wunað / þurhwunað
66.25 **perseverat** *C*

1437 86.11 mid / æt
66.25 **aput**

1438 86.11 gebana *C*, gebanum *O* / banum
66.25 **ossa**

1439 86.11 reliquium / deadum
66.25 **mortua**

1440 86.14 sęgene *C*, segene *O* / kyðinge
66.26 **narrationis**

1441 86.16 in / be
67.1 **de**

1442 86.16 geacsode / gehyrde
67.3 **audisse**

1443 86.20 fulloft *C*, fuloft *O* / gita
67.3 **usque**

1444 86.21 sæde *C*, sægde *O* / rehte
67.4 **narrat**

1445 86.23 gereorde *C*, gereordode *O* / gefyllde
67.4 **satiat**

1446 86.24 gereordnysse *C*, gereordnesse *O* / gereordunge
67.4 **refectione**

1447 86.26 wæs nama (noma *O*) / genemned
67.6 **nomine**

1448 86.31 worhton *C*, worhten *O* / gegearwodon
67.8 **fecissent**

1449 86.32 heorðbæcenne *C*, heorðbacene *O* / axbakenne
67.8 **subcinericium**

1450 87.1 þissere *C*, þisse *O* / þære
67.9 **hac**

1451 87.4 syn *C*, sin *O* / beon
67.10 *om.;* **esse** *C*

1452 87.6 wer / þeow
67.11 **famulus**

1453 87.6 þæræt / þærmid
67.11 **ad-**

1454 87.7 ongæt *C*, ongeat *O* / oncneow
67.12 **cognovit**

1455 87.9 swaþeah / eallunga
67.12 **iam**

1456 87.13 *om. C*, cwæð *O* / spræc
67.14 **dicens**

1457 87.16 þa ... sona / þærrihte
67.15 **protinus**

1458 87.17 dyde / worhte
67.15 **dedit**

1459 87.17 unmæte / ormæte
67.15 **inmensum**

1460 87.24 gedyde / worhte
67.18 **fecerat**

1461 87.24 hrine / æthrine
67.18 **contactus; tactus** *changed to* **contactus** *La*

1462 87.24 æniges / nanes

1463 87.30 haten / gehaten
67.19 **dicitur**

1464 87.30 seo / sum

1465 88.3 seo *C*, sio *O* / þe

1466 88.6 rice man (mon *O*) / hiredes hlaford
68.3 **paterfamilias**

1467 88.8 wæs / becom

1438 Hecht reported *gebænum* for *O*, querying the *æ*.

	68.3	**venisset**
1468	88.9	neah / to
	68.3	**ad**
1469	88.9	ende / endeniextan dæge
	68.3	**extremum**
1470	88.13	wære / wurde
1471	88.14	scyldum / gyltum
	68.6	**culpa**
1472	88.15	eode / ferde
	68.6	**exirit** *M*
1473	88.16	mæssepreost / sacerd
	68.7	**sacerdos**
1474	88.17	wæs / wearð
	68.7	**esset**
1475	88.17	unwenlice / unmyndlunga
	68.7	**inopinate; inpuise** *as a gloss La*
1476	88.23	hwæt / sum þing
	68.10	**aliquid**
1477	88.23	gedyde / dyde
	68.10	**fecit**
1478	88.23	hwylcehugu *C*, hwæthwega *O* / sume lytle
	68.10	**paululum**
1479	88.24	gefylde / geendode
	68.11	**expleret; implere** *M*
1480	88.25	medmyccle *C*, medmicle *O* / lytle
	68.10	**minimum**
1481	88.26	gefylled / geendod
	68.11	**expleto**
1482	88.27	feran / faran
	68.12	**pergere**
1483	88.28	7 / soðlice
	68.12	**viro** *M*
1484	88.30	geurnon / urnon
	68.12	**occurrentes**
1485	89.1	geswenced / swinc
	68.14	**fatigare**
1486	89.6	7 (ond *O*) ... swa / witodlice
	68.16	**itaque**
1487	89.8	lichaman *C*, lichoman *O* / lice
	68.16	**corpus**
1488	89.10	bære / bedde
	68.16	**lecto**
1489	89.14	semninga *C*, samninga *O* / færinga
	69.1	**repente**
1490	89.16	þærymb / þærymbuton
	69.3	**circum-**
1491	89.17	sendon *C*, sen[ ] *O* / asendum
	69.4	**-missis**
1492	89.18	wundorlicu *C*, wundorlice *O* / wundrunge
	69.3	**admirationis**
1493	89.19	gefean / blisse
	69.4	**gaudium**
1494	89.25	heora *C*, hiora *O* / þara
	69.6	**quorum**
1495	89.26	nænigra (nænige *O*) þinga / na
	69.7	**non**
1496	89.28	on / þurh
	69.7	**per**
1497	89.29	geong ... man (mon *O*) / iungling
	69.8	**iuvenis**
1498	89.31	oþrum / fiðerum
	69.9	**alis** *M*
1499	89.34	cwyþeð *C*, cweþeð *O* / bewepð
	69.10	**plangit**
1500	90.1	mæneþ / heofað
	69.10	[**plangit**]
1501	90.1	7 / soðlice
	69.10	**enim**
1502	90.3	þa / witodlice
	69.11	**scilicit** *M*
1503	90.4	cwican / geedcukedan
1504	90.7	eft acwicod (acwicad *O*) / edcukeda
	69.14	**redivivus**
1505	90.9	synnum / gyltum
	69.13	**culpis**
1506	90.10	7 *C*, ond *O* / þa
1507	90.10	geferde *C*, gewat *O* / ferde
	69.15	**exivit**
1508	90.12	gehoga ... 7 sceawa (gesceawa *O*) / besceawa
	69.15	**perpende**
1509	90.15	hine / þone
	69.16	**quem**

1490 Hecht printed *þær ymbstodon* and *þær ymbuton stodon. O*'s rubricator supplied the two letters *ær.* **1492** Hecht reported *[ ]lice* for *O.* **1497** *O*'s rubricator may have supplied the initial *g.* **1500** Both *cwyþeð* and *mæneþ*, or *bewepð* and *heofað*, render *plangit.*

1510 90.16 wære / wurde
1511 90.16 medmycelne *C*, medmicelne *O* / litelne
69.17 **modicum**
1512 90.18 wisan / þing
69.18 **haec**
1513 90.23 fundene / gemette
69.20 **inveniri**
1514 94.15 æsprynges *C*, æspringes *O* / wylles
1515 94.16 forgeofendum *C*, forgifendum *O* / þurh ... gife
1516 94.20 gehaten *C*, haten *O* / genemned
1517 94.22 sy *C*, se *O* / beon
1518 94.31 healdende 7 donde (þeonde *O*) / berende ... 7 oferstah
71.6 **gerens (regens *M*) ... transiens (proficiens *as a gloss La*)**
1519 95.1 gedafenlice *C*, gedefelice *O* / ealdlice
71.6 **senile**
1520 95.1 on / mid
1521 95.3 nænigum *C*, nænegum *O* / nanum
71.7 **nulli**
1522 95.6 lifigean *C*, lifgean *O* / freolice brucan
71.8 **libere; libere vivere, vivere *as a gloss W*$_2$**
1523 95.8 efne / eallunga
71.9 **iam**
1524 95.9 naht 7 (*om. O*) adrugod / forsearod 7 forscrunken
71.9 **aridum**
1525 95.11 cynne / kynrene
71.10 **genere**
1526 95.15 manige *C*, monig[ ] *O* / fela
71.11 **multos**
1527 95.15 gan / faran
71.12 **ire**
1528 95.16 uncysta / leahtra
71.12 **vitiorum**
1529 95.18 swa swa / swilce
71.12 **quasi**
1530 95.22 of / on
71.13 **de**
1531 95.22 geþohte 7 ungewitnysse (ond ingewitnesse *O*) / geþance
71.13 **scientia**
1532 95.23 æfter þon / syððon
72.1 **postmodum**
1533 95.24 geeode *C*, geiode *O* / ferde
72.2 **iret**
1534 95.25 7 þa *C*, 7 eac þa *O* / witodlice
72.2 **itaque**
1535 95.26 onginnum *C*, ongynnum *O* / bigengum
72.2 **studiis**
1536 95.28 licode *C*, [ ]licode *O* / gelicode
72.3 **placere**
1537 95.30 munuclifes / drohtunge
72.4 **conversionis; conversationis *C*/**
1538 95.33 snotorlice *C*, snoterlice *O* / wislice
72.5 **sapienter**
1539 96.2 godan / halgan
1540 96.3 secge / cyðe
72.6 **narro**
1541 96.3 ongæt *C*, ongeat *O* / oncneow
72.7 **agnovi**
1542 96.4 þa / þe
1543 96.5 sædon *C*, sægdun *O* / rehton
72.6 **referentibus**
1544 96.5 witodlice *C*, weotodlice *O* / þæt is
72.7 **scilicit *M***
1545 96.5 fram *C*, from *O* / æt
1546 96.7 rihtinge (ryhtinge *O*) 7 hlaforddome / ealdordome
73.1 **regimine**
1547 96.9 fram *C*, from *O* / æt
1548 96.10 fore / ealdor
73.2 **prae-**
1549 96.14 gefrægn / geaxode
72.7 [**agnovi**]
1550 96.15 fore / ealdor
73.5 **prae-**
1551 96.18 geþohte / geteohhode
73.7 **decrevissit *M***

1536 Hecht saw 'spuren von *-icode.*' Part of the *l* also remains visible. **1537** De Vogüé has reported *conversationis* for nine of the manuscripts used by Moricca; he did not see *M* (p. 333). **1549** Both *ongæt* and *gefrægn*, or *oncneow* and *geaxode*, help render *agnovi.*

1552 96.20 gesohte / secenne
73.6 **petere**
1553 96.20 westennu *C*, westen *O* / westenstowa
73.7 **deserta**
1554 96.26 arwyrðum / wurðfullum
74.1 **honestioribus**
1555 96.33 hriddern / hridder
74.3 **capisterium**
1556 97.3 sumdæl *C*, hwylcnehugu *O* / sumne dæl
1557 97.3 geclænsian / feormianne
74.2 **purgandum**
1558 97.4 þæt / hit
74.4 **quod**
1559 97.6 ungetymum / ungelimpe
74.4 **casu accedente**
1560 97.13 7 (ond *O*) þa / soðlice
74.8 **autem**
1561 97.15 wæs / wearð
1562 97.20 sona / þa eft
1563 97.20 fram *C*, from *O* / of
74.11 **ab**
1564 97.21 funde *C*, fond *O* / gemette
74.11 **repperit**
1565 97.21 neah / wið
74.11 **iuxta**
1566 97.22 gesund / gehal
74.11 **sanum**
1567 97.23 nænige *C*, ænge *O* / nane
74.12 **nulla**
1568 97.24 frefriende / gefrefrode
74.13 **consolatus**
1569 97.26 hriddern / hridder
74.13 **capisterium**
1570 97.27 gesund / gehal
74.13 **sanum**
1571 97.27 þæt / þe
74.14 **quod**
1572 97.27 nam / genam
74.14 **tulerat**
1573 97.28 seo *C*, sio *O* / þeos
74.14 **quae**
1574 97.28 wise / dæd
74.14 **res**
1575 97.29 wæs / wearð
74.14 **est**
1576 97.29 ongyten *C*, ongetenu *O* / cuð
74.15 **agnita; cognita** V_1, **reperta** *as a gloss La*
1577 97.30 eardodon *C*, eardedan *O* / wunedon
1578 97.33 hriddern / hridder
74.15 **capisterium**
1579 98.1 7 eac / ge
74.17 **et**
1580 98.1 ongætan *C*, ongean *O* / oncneowon
74.17 **agnuscerint** *M*
1581 98.3 drohtnoðes *C*, drohtoðes *O* / drohtnunge
75.1 **conversionis; conversationis** O_2
1582 98.4 fram *C*, from *O* / on
75.1 **a**
1583 98.4 swiðe / hu
75.1 **quanta**
1584 98.5 hriddern / hridder
1585 98.6 beforan / ætforan
75.2 **ante**
1586 101.3 ansyne *C*, ansine *O* / hiwe
78.25 **specie**
1587 101.4 uneaðe / earfoðlice
78.26 **vix**
1588 101.6 eac swilce (swylce *O*) / eallunga
78.27 **iam**
1589 101.7 geþreodode *C*, geþrowode *O* / þohte
78.27 **deliberaret; cogitabat** *as a gloss La*
1590 101.9 semninga *C*, sæmninga *O* / færinga
79.1 **subito**
1591 101.10 gesewen 7 gemiltsod *C*, sewen 7 gemiltsad *O* / beseah
79.1 **respectus; miserata** *as a gloss La*, **aspectu** W_2, **repletus** *Maurists, var.*
1592 101.14 ungyrede *C*, ongyrede *O* / unscrydde
79.3 **exutus**
1593 101.14 hrægle / reafe
79.3 **indumento; vestimento** *Cl*
1594 101.18 welwed *C*, wylwed *O* / gewylwed
79.4 **volutatus**

1571 *C* and *O* abbreviate ꝥ.

1595	101.22	ut gelædde / ateah
	79.6	**eduxit; duxit** V_4
1596	101.24	synlust / unlust
	79.6	**voluptatem**
1597	101.26	witodlice *C*, *def. O* / wel witelice
	79.7	**bene (***C; om. A*, **pene** *M***) poenaliter**
1598	101.29	hæte ⁊ ... synlust (syn[ ] *O*) / ontendnysse
	79.9	**incendium**
1599	101.31	þa / witodlice
	79.9	**videlicit** *M*
1600	101.32	æfter þon / syððon
	79.9	**post**
1601	101.34	synlustes / unlustes
	79.10	**voluptatis**
1602	101.34	atemed / gewyld
	79.11	**edomita**
1603	102.1	þyslices / swilces
	79.11	**tale**
1604	102.1	naht *C*, noht *O* / nan þing
	79.11	**aliquid**
1605	102.2	ongæt *C*, ongeat *O* / gefredde
	79.11	**sentirit** *M*
1606	102.3	þa / eallunga
	79.12	**iam**
1607	102.3	manige *C*, monige *O* / fela
	79.12	**multi**
1608	102.6	⁊ / cuðlice
	79.13	**quippe**
1609	102.6	uncysta *C*, uncyste *O* / leahtre
	79.13	**vitio**
1610	102.8	mid rihte / rihtlice
	79.13	**iure**
1611	102.16	hwæthugu *C*, hwæthwega *O* / be sumum dæle
	79.17	**aliquantum; aliquantulum** O_2
1612	102.17	læddan *C*, lætenan *O* / gelæddan
	79.17	**-lati**
1613	102.18	þonne hwæþre (hwæðere *O*) / swaþeah
	79.18	**tamen**
1614	102.19	gerędelicor *C*, gerædelicor *O* / fullicor
	79.18	**plenius; planius** O_2
1615	102.19	gerihted *C*, gerecced *O* / getrahtnod
	79.18	**exponi**
1616	102.24	witodlice / soðlice
	79.21	**autem**
1617	102.26	forþon / eornostlice
	79.22	**ergo; autem** *Bo*
1618	102.29	syn *C*, sin *O* / beon
	79.22	**-esse**
1619	102.31	syn *C*, sin *O* / beon
1620	102.31	gewinnum / geswinceum
	79.23	**laboribus-**
1621	102.32	æfter (ofer *O*) þæt / eallunga
	79.23	**viro (***M***) iam**
1622	103.7	unluce *C*, onluce *O* / geopenodest
	80.2	**reserasti**
1623	103.19	soðlice / genihtsumne
	80.5	**feracius; veracius** *later hand A*, **perfectius** *as a gloss La*
1624	103.20	godra / haligra
	80.5	**virtutum**
1625	103.20	weorca / mægna
	80.5	**[virtutum]**
1626	103.21	þæs / his
	80.7	**eius**
1627	103.21	lifes / drohtnunge
	80.6	**conversationis**
1628	103.22	wæs / wearð
1629	103.22	gemærsod / gehæfd mære
	80.7	**celebre (***C;* **sollempniter** *as a gloss La***) ... habebatur**
1630	103.23	naht feorr *C*, noht feor *O* / unfeorr
	80.7	**non longe**
1631	103.24	*om. C*, fæder *O* / ealdor
	80.8	**pater**
1632	103.26	comon *C*, cwom *O* / becom
	80.9	**venit**
1633	103.30	fore / ealdor
	80.10	**prae-**
1634	103.32	beforan / fore
	80.12	**prae-**
1635	104.1	sealde geþafunge / getiðode
	80.12	**adsensum dedit**
1636	104.2	nam *C*, nom *O* / heold

1612 Hecht printed *forðlæddan*, *forðlætenan*, and *forð gelæddan*. **1625** Both *godra weorca* and *haligra mægna* render *virtutum*. **1634** Hecht printed *beforan sæde* and *foresæde*.

80.13 **tenerit** *M*
1637 104.2 hyrdnysse *C*, hiordnisse *O* / gehealdsumnysse
80.13 **custodiam**
1638 104.5 nænigum *C*, nænegum *O* / nanum
80.14 **nulli-**
1639 104.6 unalyfedan / unalyfedlice
80.14 **inlicitos**
1640 104.7 munuclifes *C*, munoclifes *O* / munuclicre drohtnunge
80.15 **conversationis**
1641 104.9 gebroðru *C*, gebroðro *O* / broðro
80.16 **fratres**
1642 104.12 þæt / forþam þe
80.17 **quia**
1643 104.13 fore / ealdor
80.17 **prae-**
1644 104.14 bealh *C*, bealg *O* / ætspearn
80.18 **offendebat**
1645 104.14 for / æt
80.18 **in**
1646 104.14 þeawum / regole
80.18 **norma; regula** *as a gloss La*
1647 104.15 rihtwisnysse *C*, rihtwisnesse *O* / rihtinge
80.18 **rectitudinis; aequitate** *as a gloss La*
1648 104.17 weorc *C*, worc *O* / þing
1649 104.17 worhton / donne
1650 104.19 sorgodon / besargodon
80.19 **dolerent**
1651 104.20 þuhte / wæs
80.20 **essit** *M*
1652 104.21 healdlic *C*, heardlic *O* / heard
80.20 **durum-**
1653 104.21 genydede *C*, genyded *O* / geneadode
80.20 **cogebantur**
1654 104.22 eallum / ealdum
80.20 **veteri**
1655 104.23 wisan / þing
1656 104.26 ongunnon ... trahtian (trahtigean *O*) / þohton
81.1 **tractare ... conati (meditati** *as a gloss La***)**
1657 104.27 hwæthugu *C*, hwæthwega *O* / sum þing
81.1 **aliquid**
1658 104.30 glæsfæt *C*, glæs[ ] *O* / glæsene fæt
81.2 **vas vitreum**
1659 104.31 wolberenda *C*, [ ]da *O* / deadberenda
81.3 **pestifer**
1660 104.32 arwurþan / halgan
1661 104.33 swa swa *C*, *def. O* / æfter
81.3 **ex**
1662 104.34 mynstres / mynsterlicum
81.3 **monasterii**
1663 105.4 þegnunge *C*, senunge *O* / tacne
81.6 **signo**
1664 105.5 wæs / wearð
81.6 **est**
1665 105.6 mid ... wurpe *C*, sende *O* / asende
81.7 **dedissit** *M*
1666 105.7 forwyrde / deaðes
81.6 **mortis**
1667 105.9 ongæt *C*, onget *O* / undergeat
81.7 **intellexit**
1668 105.12 þa hraðe (raðe *O*) / þærrihte
81.9 **ilico**
1669 105.14 gecigde / gelangode
81.9 **convocatus**
1670 105.19 *om. C*, and *O* / hu
81.11 **quid; nunquid** V_1
1671 105.21 an wise / ætgædere
81.12 **con-**
1672 105.21 gað / farað
81.13 **ite**
1673 105.23 fæder 7 hlaford / ealdor
81.13 **patrem**
1674 105.24 nan þing *C*, nænige þincga *O* / na
81.14 **menime**

1642 *C* abbreviates ꝥ. **1656** Both versions of the translation also use *smeagean(ne)* here to help render *tractare* or *conati*. **1658** Hecht reported *O* as defective. **1668** Hecht gave *statim* for the Latin (*Einleitung*, p. 165), yet his only acknowledged source, the Maurists' printed edition, has *illico*. Cf. entries **278** and **2426**. **1670** De Vogüé has reported *numquid* for *A* (p. 331; cited incorrectly as on 81.10). **1674** De Vogüé has reported *minime* for *A* (p. 329, n. 13).

1675 105.24 ofer / æfter
81.14 **post**

1676 105.27 anetnysse *C*, ænetnesse *O* / ænettes
81.15 **solitudinis**

1677 105.30 naht *C*, noht *O* / na
81.17 **minus**

1678 105.34 gebroðra *C*, gebroðru *O* / broðro

1679 106.1 spelliende / wordliende
81.19 **conspirantes**

1680 106.2 liflade / drohtnunge
81.20 **conversationis**

1681 106.2 swiðe / feorran
81.20 **longe**

1682 106.3 genyded *C*, geneded *O* / geneadod
81.20 **coactus**

1683 106.6 stiþnysse *C*, stiðnesse *O* / stiðlican drohtnunge
81.21 **vigoris usum**

1684 106.10 sceawunge / besceawunge
81.22 **contemplationis**

1685 106.10 daga gehwilce (gehwylce *O*) / dæghwamlice
81.23 **cottidiae** *M*

1686 106.12 gymde *C*, *def. O* / begymde
81.24 **curaret**

1687 106.13 þearfa *C*, ðearfe *O* / lif
81.24 *om.;* **vitam** *Bo*

1688 106.15 gelærde / gerihtlæhte
81.25 **invenirit** *M*

1689 106.17 fram *C*, buton *O* / wiðutan
81.26 **extra**

1690 106.21 gehygd *C*, ingehyd *O* / geþanc

1691 106.23 wisan / þing

1692 106.27 forname *C*, fornome *O* / forspillde
82.2 **consumpsit**

1693 106.28 yrfes / æhta

1694 106.30 fedde / læsode
82.3 **pavit**

1695 106.31 þa / hy
82.3 **quos**

1696 106.31 þa / 7
82.4 **et; cum** V_2

1697 106.33 æfter þan (ðon *O*) / syððon
82.4 **postmodum**

1698 107.2 wære / wearð

1699 107.3 manig *C*, monige *O* / fela
82.6 **quanti**

1700 107.5 genihtsumað / habbað ... genohne
82.6 **habundant**

1701 107.6 ac nu / gewisslice
82.7 **igitur**

1702 107.8 forþon / eornostlice
82.8 **ergo**

1703 107.12 heordnysse *C*, heordnesse *O* / gehealdsumnysse
82.9 **custodia**

1704 107.13 sceawode / besceawode
82.10 **aspiciens**

1705 107.14 smeagende / ameriende
82.10 **examinans**

1706 107.16 aflymde ne ... abygde (gebigde *O*) / gewidmærsode
82.11 **devulgavit; elongavit** *Maurists, var.*

1707 107.16 fram *C*, buton *O* / wiðutan
82.10 **extra**

1708 107.18 la / ac
82.12 **ergo**

1709 107.22 carcerne / cwearterne
82.13 **carcere**

1710 107.24 sænde *C*, sende *O* / asende
82.14 **misit**

1711 107.26 bade / geanbidunge
82.15 **expectatione**

1712 107.29 butan / wiðutan
82.17 **extra**

1713 107.30 gewitað / gelædde
82.18 **recedimus; reducimur** *Bo*, **ducimur** *Cl*, **deicimur** *as a gloss* Pa_2

1714 108.2 þonne *C*, þone *O* / ac
82.21 **vero**

1715 108.2 þes / se
82.21 **iste**

1716 108.4 ellhygd *C*, hellehygd *O* / wafunge
82.22 **extasi**

1680 De Vogüé has reported *conversationi* for all the manuscripts used by Moricca, with the possible exception of *M* (p. 333). **1682** De Vogüé has reported *coactos* for *A* (p. 331). **1683** Both versions also use *gewunan* here to help render *usum.* **1714** Hecht reported *þonne* for *O.*

1717 108.4 buton *C*, butan *O* / wiðutan
82.22 **extra**
1718 108.5 swaþeh *C*, swaðeah *O* / þeah
82.22 **quidem; equidem *C***
1719 108.6 of / ofer
82.22 **super; supra *La***
1720 108.6 forþon / eornostlice
82.23 **ergo**
1721 108.8 gegaderode *C*, gegearwode *O* / geteah
82.24 **collegit**
1722 108.10 for / fram
82.23 **ab**
1723 108.10 gedwolan / gedwylde
82.23 **errore**
1724 108.10 swa eac / ⁊
82.24 **et**
1725 108.26 cuþ / licað
83.5 **placet; patit *M***
1726 108.27 ⁊swarige *C*, ⁊swạrie *O* / secge
83.5 **respondeas**
1727 108.31 þær þe *C*, þær *O* / þærþær
83.7 **ibi; ubi *changed to* ibi W_2 *or* 83.8 ubi**
1728 108.32 aberene ⁊ ... adreoganne *C*, aberenne ⁊ ... adreogenne *O* / forberenne
83.8 **portandi; tolerandi *La***
1729 109.2 þær þe *C*, þær *O* / þærþær
83.9 **ubi**
1730 109.5 gewinn / geswinc
83.10 **labor**
1731 109.7 genihtsumiað ... ⁊ gefultumiaþ *C*, genihtsumað ... ⁊ gefultumað *O* / gestrangiað
83.11 **subpetant *M***
1732 109.8 wisan / þing
83.10 **causae**
1733 109.9 betran *C*, beteran *O* / selran
83.11 **meliorem**
1734 109.12 gestod / stod
83.12 **staret**
1735 109.15 witodlice ([ ]ice *O*) swa / ⁊
83.13 **et**
1736 109.15 hit / þæt
1737 109.15 fulloft *C*, fuloft *O* / foroft
83.13 **saepe**
1738 109.17 swigunge / swigean
83.14 **silentio**
1739 109.18 ⁊ *C*, ðæt *O* / forþam
83.14 **quia**
1740 109.19 gewin *C*, gewinn *O* / geswinc
83.15 **laborem**
1741 109.21 gewinne / geswince
83.16 **laborem**
1742 109.21 be þan (þon *O*) / ðanon
83.16 **unde**
1743 109.23 wilnige *C*, wilnie *O* / gewilnode
83.17 **cupit**
1744 109.28 nalæs *C*, nallæs *O* / na
83.19 **non**
1745 109.30 þus *C*, þas *O* / þa þing
83.19 **haec**
1746 109.30 aræfnienne *C*, ræfnienne *O* / forberene
83.19 **toleranda**
1747 109.32 þa / hi
1748 109.32 gedyglian ⁊ ... bebeorgan *C*, gedigean ⁊ ... bebyrgean *O* / forbugan
83.20 **evadere**
1749 110.1 spertan / wylian
83.21 **sportam-**
1750 110.2 ofdune / nyðer
83.21 **de-**
1751 110.2 aseted / alæten
83.22 **-poni**
1752 110.4 þæt / hwæðer
83.22 **num-**
1753 110.5 cyþende / sæde
83.23 **testatur**
1754 110.10 gewin *C*, gewinn *O* / geswinc
83.25 **laborem**
1755 110.11 gewinne / geswince
83.25 **laborem**
1756 110.13 ⁊ (ond *O*) swa / soþlice
83.26 **enim; etenim *C***
1757 110.14 wiga / fyhtling
83.26 **praeliator**
1758 110.16 campes / gecampes

1725 De Vogüé has reported *patet* for *A* (p. 331). **1727** *CO's þær (þe)* renders *ibi* (83.7, var. *ubi*); *H's þærþær, ubi* (83.8).

83.26 **certaminis**

1759 110.18 bealdlice *C*, heardlice *O* / hrædlice

84.2 **citius**

1760 110.20 cwic / libbende

84.2 **viros; vivus *M***

1761 110.21 ungelæredlican *C*, ungeræd-lican *O* / earfoðlæran

84.2 **indociles**

1762 110.22 manige *C*, monige *O* / fela

84.3 **quantos; tot V_1**

1763 113.20 stæþe *C*, staðe *O* / ofre

89.7 **ripam**

1764 113.21 wæterseaðes / wæteres seaðes

89.7 **laci**

1765 113.26 ahleop / ræsde

89.9 **-siliens**

1766 113.27 gefeoll / befeoll

89.9 **cecidit**

1767 113.28 witodlice / swa

89.9 **scilicit *M***

1768 113.29 nænig / nan

89.11 **nulla**

1769 114.1 wen / hiht

89.10 **spes**

1770 114.1 geloman / isene tol

89.10 **ferramenti *C***

1771 114.1 ofer þæt / eallunga

89.11 **iam**

1772 114.2 swa / witodlice

89.11 **itaque**

1773 114.2 forlorenum / forspilledum

89.11 **perdito**

1774 114.4 bodode / cyðde

89.12 **nuntiavit**

1775 114.6 gehet / dyde

89.13 **egit**

1776 114.6 scylde / gyltes

89.13 **reatus**

1777 114.6 dædbote / behreowsunge

89.13 **poenitentiam**

1778 114.7 þæt / hit

89.13 **quod**

1779 114.8 secgan / cyðde

89.14 **indicare; dicere *M***

1780 114.9 7 *C*, ond *O* / hwæt

89.14 **igitur; itaque O_2, autem *C*/**

1781 114.11 eode *C*, iode *O* / stop

89.15 **accessit**

1782 114.12 on / of

89.15 **de**

1783 114.13 þa hraþe (raðe *O*) / þærrihte

89.16 **mox**

1784 114.14 gecyrde ... eft / gehwearf ... 7 wearð

89.17 **rediit adque (*M*) ... intravit**

1785 114.15 sona / hrædlice

89.17 **statim**

1786 114.17 geloman *C*, bill *O* / tol

89.18 **ferramentum**

1787 114.18 geloma *C*, bill *O* / tol

1788 114.19 ofer þis / nan þing

1789 114.20 geunrotsod *C*, geunrotsad *O* / sari

89.18 **contristari**

1790 114.24 wæs / wunode

89.21 **consisterit *M***

1791 114.24 mynstre / cyricean

89.21 **cella**

1792 114.25 gangende / agan

89.22 **-gressus**

1793 114.26 cniht / cnapa

89.21 **puer**

1794 114.28 forlet / nyðer alet

89.23 **submittens**

1795 114.31 gefeoll / feallende ... fyliende

89.23 **cadendo secutus**

1796 114.32 underfeng / gegrap

90.1 **rapuit**

1797 114.32 teah *C*, *def. O* / ateah

90.2 **traxit; retraxit *Bo***

1798 114.33 ofdunewheardes / innor

90.2 **introrsus**

1799 114.34 fullneah *C*, fulneah *O* / nealice

90.1 **paene**

1800 115.1 drihtnes / godes

90.2 **dei**

1801 115.2 mynstre / cyrcean

90.3 **cellam**

1802 115.3 sona / hrædlice

1760 De Vogüé has reported *vivos* for nine of the manuscripts used by Moricca, all but *M* (p. 333).
1777 De Vogüé has reported *paenitentiam* for *A* (p. 329). **1792** Hecht printed *utgangende* and *ut agan*.

	90.3	**protinus**
1803	115.3	cigde / clypode
	90.3	**vocavit**
1804	115.6	cniht / cnapa
	90.4	**puer**
1805	115.6	eode / ferde
	90.5	**perrexerat**
1806	115.7	nu / eallunga
	90.5	**iam-**
1807	115.8	ofdune / aweg
	90.5	**longius**
1808	115.9	þæt / hu
1809	115.9	þæt / þær
1810	115.9	wæs / geweard
1811	115.10	wise / þing
	90.6	**res**
1812	115.11	swiðe / [hu]
1813	115.12	hwæt (þæt *O*) ... þa / soðlice
	90.7	**etenim**
1814	115.14	þære / hyre
1815	115.14	hræd / hrædlice
	90.8	**concitus; concite *CI***
1816	115.15	æfter / be
	90.7	**ad**
1817	115.15	fæder / ealdres
	90.7	**patris**
1818	115.17	cniht / cnapan
	90.9	**puer**
1819	115.17	yþe / stream
	90.9	**unda**
1820	115.18	ofer / uppon
	90.10	**super**
1821	115.19	ofer / on
	90.9	**per**
1822	115.20	genam ***C***, genom ***O*** / gelæhte
	90.10	**tenuit**
1823	115.20	cniht / cnapan
1824	115.21	loccum / feaxe
	90.10	**capillos**
1825	115.21	færlicum ***C***, færlice ***O*** / swiftum
	90.11	**rapido**
1826	115.23	wæs ***C, def. O*** / wearð
1827	115.28	ferde / arn ... gewurde
	90.12	**cucurrissit ... fierit (*M*)**
1828	115.28	wæs / wearð
1829	115.29	wundriende / mid wundrunge
	90.13	**miratus**
1830	115.29	wisan / dæde
	90.14	**factum**
1831	115.29	aforhtode ***C***, forhtode ***O*** / afyrht
	90.14	**extremuit; expavit *C*, extimuit *later hand* V_2**
1832	115.30	fædær ***C***, fæder ***O*** / ealdre
	90.14	**patrem**
1833	115.30	gesæde ***C***, asægde ***O*** / rehte
	90.14	**retulit; narravit V_2**
1834	115.31	wisan / þing
	90.14	**rem**
1835	115.32	witodlice / þa
	90.15	**autem**
1836	115.32	halga / arwurða
	90.15	**venerabilis; domini venerabilis *C*, domini Pa_1**
1837	115.33	***om. C***, on ***O*** / to
1838	115.34	***om. C***, [on ***O***] / to
1839	116.1	7 (ond ***O***) þa / ac
	90.16	**at; ac *Bo*, atque *Ta***
1840	116.1	ongæn (ongen ***O***) hine / þærongean
	90.16	**contra; e contra *Maurists***
1841	116.4	nænig / na
	90.18	**non**
1842	116.5	þæt ***C, om. O*** / þe
	90.18	**quam**
1843	116.5	dyde / worhte
	90.18	**fecissit *M***
1844	116.8	þær ... to / þærto
	90.19	**ac-**
1845	116.8	eode ***C***, geeode ***O*** / genealæhte
	90.19	**-cessit**
1846	116.9	cniht / cnapa
	90.19	**puer**
1847	116.12	atogen ***C, def. O*** / getogen
	90.20	**traherer**
1848	116.14	þa ylcan ***C***, [ ]ne ilcan ***O*** / hine sylfne
	90.21	**ipsum**

1812 *CO* has *þæt ... wundorlicu ... 7 ... swiðe ungewunelicu* beside *H*'s *hu wundorlic ... 7 ... ungewunelic.* **1832** Hecht reported *fædær* for *O.* **1838** *H* repeats the preposition *to, O* uses *on* only once, and *C* does not have a preposition. **1840** The Maurists printed *econtra.* **1842** *C* abbreviates *ꝥ.* **1848** When undamaged

1849 116.15 gelædan / teon
90.21 **-ducere**
1850 116.16 wundorlice 7 myccle *C*, wunderlice 7 micle *O* / mære
90.23 **magna; mira** *as a gloss* Pa_2
1851 116.17 wisan / þing
1852 116.21 swyþor *C*, swiððor *O* / ma
90.24 **plus**
1853 116.24 7swarode / cwæð
1854 116.24 midty þe / ða þa
90.26 **cum**
1855 116.27 naman *C*, noman *O* / lufe
90.26 **amore**
1856 116.29 manige *C*, monige *O* / fela
91.1 **multi**
1857 117.5 goddæde *C*, goddæda *O* / mægenes god
91.3 **virtutis bono**
1858 117.6 ær *C*, no ðy ær *O* / ne
91.4 **non**
1859 117.7 willað *C*, wyllað *O* / gewilniað
91.4 **appetunt**
1860 117.11 hete 7 ... niðe / yfelnysse
91.6 **malitia**
1861 117.12 gehrinen / þurhslagen
91.6 **perculsus; percussus** *Hf*
1862 117.14 willan 7 geornnysse (gyrnesse *O*) / gecneordnyssum
91.6 **studiis**
1863 117.15 liflade / drohtnunge
91.7 **conversationi**
1864 117.15 swa hwylcum ... swa / gehwylce ... þe
91.7 **quosque**
1865 117.16 wolde / ongan
1866 117.16 gestyran 7 (ond *O*) (...) læran / geweman
91.8 **conpescere**
1867 117.17 þa *C*, *om.* *O* / eac
91.7 **-iam**
1868 117.18 æfæstiga *C*, æfæsta *O* / niðfulla
1869 117.19 wiðwiþerian *C*, wiðwiðeran *O* / wiðstandan
91.9 **obviare**
1870 117.20 mannes *C*, monnes *O* / weres
1871 117.20 fram ænigum *C*, fremmingum *O* / forðweardnysse
91.9 **provectibus; provectionibus** Pa_1
1872 117.23 godan / mæran
1873 117.23 lifes / drohtnunge
91.9 **conversationis**
1874 117.24 unablinnendlice / untolætendlice
91.11 **indesinenter**
1875 117.25 þæs ylcan (ilcan *O*) / his
91.11 **eius**
1876 117.27 wæs / wearð
1877 117.27 a ma 7 ma / swyðor 7 swyðor
91.12 **magis magisque (ac magis** *Cl***)**
1878 117.28 þyccylum *C*, þæcelum *O* / blæsum
91.12 **facibus**
1879 117.28 æfæste *C*, æfestunge *O* / niðes
91.11 **invidiae**
1880 117.28 getihted *C*, getiht[ ] *O* / tælde
91.12 **deterior**
1881 117.31 herenesse *C*, [ ]ere[ ]e *O* / herunge
91.13 **laudem**
1882 117.32 þæs / his
91.13 **illius**
1883 117.32 clænan / mæran
1884 117.32 lifes / drohtnunge
91.12 **conversationis**
1885 118.1 wæs / wearð
1886 118.2 æfæste *C*, æfstunge *O* / andan
91.14 **invidiae**
1887 118.5 godes / drihtnes
91.15 **domini; dei** Pa_2
1888 118.6 beweledne (bewelledne *O*) ... 7 mid attre gemengedne / geættrodne
91.15 **infectum (mixtum** *as a gloss La***) veneno**
1889 118.8 onfeng / underfeng
91.17 **suscipit**
1890 118.8 drihtnes / godes
91.17 **dei; domini** *Bo*
1891 118.9 7 *C*, ond *O* / ac
91.17 **sed**
1892 118.10 bemiþen / forholen

O presumably read *þone ilcan.* **1880** Hecht reported *getih[ ]* for *O. CO*'s *wyrsa* also may render *deterior.* **1881** Hecht reported *O* as defective.

91.18 **latuit**
1893 118.10 wol / cwalu
91.17 **pestis**
1894 118.10 þæt / þe
91.17 **quae**
1895 118.11 tihhode *C*, tihcode *O* / gemynt
1896 118.12 ac / soþlice
91.18 **viro**
1897 118.13 on / to
91.18 **ad**
1898 118.13 tide ... gereordnysse (gereordnesse *O*) / gereordungtide
91.18 **horam ... refectionis**
1899 118.16 of / æt
91.19 **de**
1900 118.17 fugel *C*, fugol *O* / hrefn
1901 118.17 mid / swa
92.1 **cum**
1902 118.17 gewunelican þeawe / gewuna
92.1 **more solito**
1903 118.20 æfestiga *C*, æfstigea *O* / niðfulla
1904 118.22 his / þæs
1905 118.23 nim / genim
92.3 **tolle**
1906 118.27 untyndum *C*, ontyndum *O* / openum
92.5 **aperto**
1907 118.29 ymb *C*, ymbe *O* / ymbutan
92.5 **circa**
1908 118.30 emne swa / swilce
92.6 **ac si**
1909 123.14 nænigne *C*, nænige *O* / nane
97.6 **nullum**
1910 123.18 godcundan / godes
97.7 **dei**
1911 123.22 ofdune / neoðor
97.8 **altius**
1912 123.24 feondgyld *C*, feondgild *O* / deofolgyld
97.9 **idolum**
1913 123.24 þæt / hit
97.9 **quo**
1914 123.25 in / into
97.9 **in**
1915 123.26 semninga *C*, sæmninga *O* / færinga
97.10 **repente**
1916 123.26 geþuht / gesewen
97.10 **visus**
1917 123.27 þær ... ut / þærof
97.10 **ex-; ex- ... de eo** V_2
1918 123.27 þæt / hit
1919 123.29 getimbre / getimbrung
97.12 **aedificium**
1920 123.30 fornumen / forburnen
97.12 **consumeretur**
1921 123.32 swa / swylce
97.13 **quasi**
1922 124.1 dwæscað *C*, dwæsceað *O* / adwæscenne
97.13 **extinguendo**
1923 124.1 wæs *C*, *def. O* / wearð
1924 124.2 godes / drihtnes
97.14 **domini; dei** Pa_1
1925 124.3 fram *C*, fore *O* / mid
97.13 *om.;* **ab** W_2
1926 124.3 com (cwom *O*) ... to / becom
97.14 **advenit**
1927 124.6 7 / ac
1928 124.7 gesewen *C*, gesewen 7 ongiten *O* / oncnawen
1929 124.7 hraðe *C*, raðe *O* / hrædlice
97.15 **protinus**
1930 124.8 to / on
97.15 **in**
1931 124.9 to / ongean
97.17 **re-;** *om. A*
1932 124.10 scinlacan / gedwimorlicum
97.16 **phantastico; phantasmatico** V_4, **inani** *as a gloss La*
1933 124.11 bysmrian / bepæhte
97.16 **deludi**
1934 124.13 hus / getimbrung
97.18 **aedificium**
1935 124.15 beheoldon *C*, behioldon *O* / gesawon
97.19 **viderent**
1936 124.20 þæs / sumes
1937 124.22 neodþearflicu (nedþearflicu *O*) wise / neode

1894 *C* and *O* abbreviate ꝥ. **1913** De Vogüé has reported *quod* for *A* (p. 331); a reading confirmed by Zimmermann's facsimile of the manuscript page (pl. 15).

97.20 **res**
1938 124.24 locum / clysingum
97.22 **claustra**
1939 124.25 willan 7 geornnysse (geornesse *O*) / geornfulnysse
97.21 **studio**
1940 124.26 *om. C,* þam *O* / him
97.22 **cui**
1941 124.28 feran / gecuman
97.23 **pergerit**
1942 124.28 to / mid
97.23 **ad**
1943 124.29 worhton / swincendum
97.23 **laborantes**
1944 124.30 sona ... hrædlice / swiftlice
97.24 **celerrime**
1945 124.30 bebead *C,* onbead *O* / cyðde
97.24 **nuntiavit; indicavit** ***C***
1946 124.31 broðrum / gebroðrum
97.24 **fratribus**
1947 124.33 cymþ *C, def. O* / becymð
98.2 **venit**
1948 125.1 on ... for *C,* [ ]r lædde *O* / þyder brohte
98.2 **detulit**
1949 125.5 fylle / hryre
98.5 **ruina**
1950 125.6 forþryccende *C,* forðriccende *O* / ofþryccende
98.5 **oppraemens** ***M;*** **comprimens** O_2
1951 125.6 geþræste *C,* geðr[ ]ste *O* / tocwysde
98.5 **conteruit**
1952 125.7 muneca *C,* muneca ... cniht *O* / munuccnapan
98.4 **puerolum (*M*) monachum**
1953 125.8 wæron *C,* wæ[ ]n *O* / wurdon
98.5 *om.;* **sunt** ***CI***
1954 125.10 geunrotsode *C,* ge[ ]rotsode *O* / geunrette
98.5 **contristati**
1955 125.12 geþræstednysse *C,* geþræstnesse *O* / tocwysednysse
98.6 **contritione**
1956 125.14 heofe *C,* heafe *O* / wope
98.7 **luctu**
1957 125.14 bodian *C,* gebodian *O* / kyðanne
98.8 **nuntiare**
1958 125.17 gewundodan / forwundedan
98.8 **delaceratum**
1959 125.18 cniht / cnapan
98.8 **puerum; puerulum** ***C***
1960 125.18 þa *C, def. O* / ac
1961 125.21 nalæs *C,* nalles *O* / na
98.10 **non**
1962 125.22 tobræcan *C, def. O* / tocwysdon
98.11 **contriverant; triverant** V_3**, contrita sunt** ***Bo***
1963 125.23 gebrysedon *C,* gebrysdon *O* / tobrysdon
98.11 [**contriverant; triverant** V_3**, contrita sunt** ***Bo***]
1964 125.24 sona / þærrihte
98.11 **statim**
1965 125.26 on / uppon
98.12 **in**
1966 125.27 on / onuppan
1967 125.27 sænde *C,* sende *O* / asendum
98.13 **missis-; dimissis-** W_2
1968 125.29 gefealh / befealh
98.14 **incubuit; accubuit** V_2
1969 125.31 wise / þing
98.14 **res**
1970 125.32 þæt / þær
1971 125.32 wæs / gewearð
1972 125.33 cniht / cnapan
1973 126.2 gegearwian 7 (ond *O*) fulfremman / fullgearwian
98.16 **perficerit**
1974 126.4 broþrum / gebroðrum
98.16 **fratribus**
1975 126.4 mid / be
98.17 **de**
1976 126.7 betweoh *C,* betwih *O* / betwux
98.19 **inter**
1977 126.8 wisum / þingum
98.19 **ista**
1978 126.9 mid / on
1979 126.9 witedomes / witegunge
98.19 **prophetiae**

1941 De Vogüé has reported *pergere(n)t* for *A* (p. 329). **1951** Hecht reported *gedr[ ]ste* for *O.*
1963 Both *tobræcan* and *gebrysedon,* or *tocwysdon* and *tobrysdon,* render *contriverant.*

1980 126.10 bodode / foresæde
98.20 **praedicere**
1981 126.11 sægde / cyðde
98.21 **nuntiare; denuntiare** Pa_2**, narrare** ***Maurists, var.***
1982 126.15 broðra *C*, broðor *O* / gebroðru
98.23 **fratres**
1983 126.16 eodon / ferdon
98.23 **-grederentur**
1984 126.16 7sware *C*, ondsware *O* / spræce
98.22 **responsum**
1985 126.17 namon ne ... þigdon mete ne drync (oððe drinc *O*) / æton ne druncon
98.23 **cibum (*C*) potumque ... sumerent**
1986 126.18 wiðutan *C*, butan *O* / ut of
98.23 **extra**
1987 126.19 midty þe *C*, *def. O* / ða þa
99.1 **cumque**
1988 126.20 for / be
99.1 **de**
1989 126.20 ymbhydiglican *C*, ymbehydigli[ ] *O* / carfullice
99.1 **sollicite**
1990 126.22 eodon / ferdon
99.2 **-gressi**
1991 126.24 wæron / wurdon
99.3 **sunt**
1992 126.24 genydde *C*, geneðde *O* / geneadode
99.3 **conpulsi**
1993 126.25 for / oð
1994 126.27 wicodon / wunode
99.3 **manere**
1995 126.29 namon ... mete 7 þigdon / ætan
99.4 **sumpserunt cibum (*C*)**
1996 126.30 cyrdon *C*, cirdon *O* / gecyrdon
99.5 **-issent**
1997 127.4 sona / hrædlice
99.6 **protinus**
1998 127.10 in / into
99.9 **in-**
1999 127.13 druncon / gedruncon
99.11 **bibistis**
2000 127.13 manige *C*, monige *O* / fela
99.10 **tot**
2001 127.14 calicas *C*, caliceas *O* / scencea
99.10 **calices**
2002 127.15 rehte / sæde
99.13 **dicerit *M***
2003 127.17 rim / getel
99.12 **numerum**
2004 127.17 gecneowon *C*, gecnewon *O* / oncneowon
99.13 **recognuscentes *M***
2005 127.18 sona / þa
2006 127.21 gegylt *C*, gylt *O* / agylt
99.14 **deliquisse**
2007 127.23 scylde / gylte
99.15 **culpam**
2008 127.23 gehogodon *C*, geheton *O* / þencende
99.15 **perpendens**
2009 127.26 ongæton *C*, ongeaton *O* / wiston
99.16 **scirent**
2010 127.34 for / ferde
99.20 **venire**
2011 128.9 wegfereld *C*, wegfer[ ] *O* / wegferend
99.22 **viator; conviator** V_3
2012 128.11 mettas to þicgenne in ... wege (ðicge[ ]ege *O*) / formete
99.22 **sumendos in itenere ... cibos (*C*)**
2013 128.17 þicgan mete / etan
99.24 **sumamus cibum (*C*)**
2014 128.19 þam / him
99.24 **cui**
2015 128.19 feorr *C*, feor *O* / ne
99.25 **ab-**
2016 128.22 com / becom
99.26 **venire; pervenire *Ta***
2017 128.26 gefremedon / geferdon
100.2 **egissent; peregissent *Bo***
2018 128.27 medmycelne *C*, medmicelne *O* / sumne
100.2 **aliquantulum**
2019 128.28 lærde / mynegode
100.2 **admonuit**
2020 128.29 heran *C*, hyran *O* / geþwærian

1982 In the 'Berichtigungen' to his edition (after p. 374), Hecht renumbered lines 15-30 of p. 126.
2010 Both versions also use *becom* here to help render *venire.*

	100.3	**consentire**
2021	128.29	se / he
	100.3	**qui**
2022	128.30	getihhode / teohhode
	100.3	**decreverat; consueverat** ***M***
2023	128.34	ferde / farenne
	100.5	**pergere**
2024	128.34	geþafode / geþwærode
	100.5	**consensit**
2025	129.2	ufere / lætre
	100.6	**tardior**
2026	129.2	geswencte / gewæhte
	100.6	**fatigaret**
2027	129.3	in / be
	100.7	**in**
2028	129.4	fægre ***C***, fægere ***O*** / wynsumne
2029	129.4	easpryng ***C***, æsprincg ***O*** / wylle
	100.7	**fontem**
2030	129.7	mid / to
	100.8	**ad**
2031	129.10	þis / her
2032	129.10	fægru ***C***, fægeru ***O*** / smeðe
	100.9	**amoenus**
2033	129.12	æfter þon / syððan
	100.11	**postmodum**
2034	129.13	onsunde ***C***, onsundne ***O*** / gesunde
	100.11	**incolomes**
2035	129.13	gefaran / faran
	100.11	**explere**
2036	129.14	midþy ***C***, mitty ***O*** / witodlice þa
	100.11	**cum igitur (ergo V_2)**
2037	129.17	manunge ***C***, monuncge ***O*** / mynegunge
	100.12	**admonitione**
2038	129.17	gehyrde ***C***, hirde ***O*** / getiðode
	100.13	**consensit**
2039	129.20	gecyðed ***C***, geondweardod ond gecyðed ***O*** / becom beforan
	100.14	**praesentatus**
2040	129.22	gewilnode ***C***, gew[ ] ***O*** / bæd
	100.15	**petiit**
2041	129.24	godes ***C***, gode[ ] ***O*** / halga
	100.15	**sanctus**
2042	129.28	se / þe
	100.17	**qui**
2043	129.29	se / he
2044	129.31	æftran ***C***, æfteran ***O*** / oðre
	100.18	**secundo**
2045	129.34	ongæt ***C***, ongeat ***O*** / oncneow
	100.20	**agnuscens** ***M***
2046	130.1	scylde / gylt
	100.19	**reatum**
2047	130.2	forð onloten / gebigde
	100.20	**provolutus**
2048	130.3	mannes ***C***, monnes ***O*** / weres
2049	130.3	ma / swyðor
	100.21	**magis**
2050	130.4	scylde / gylt
	100.21	**culpam**
2051	130.4	weopan ***C***, wepan ***O*** / bewepan
	100.21	**deflere**
2052	130.7	beforan / on
	100.22	**in**
2053	130.7	his / þæs
2054	130.7	eagum / gesihðe
	100.22	**oculis**
2055	130.9	þyses ***C***, þises ***O*** / þæs
2056	130.11	he / se
	100.24	**qui**
2057	130.12	þegne / leorningcnihte
	100.24	**discipulo**
2058	130.14	7swarode / cwæð
2059	130.16	þrage / hwile
	101.1	**interim**
2060	130.16	ofer þis / nu gyta
	101.2	**adhuc**
2061	130.17	wisan / þing
2062	130.17	ongytan ***C***, ongitan ***O*** / oncnawan
	101.2	**cognuscas** ***M;*** **agnoscas** ***CI***
2063	130.20	witedomes / witegunge
	101.4	**prophetiae**
2064	130.22	naht feor ***C***, noht feorr ***O*** / unfeorr
	101.5	**paulo longius**
2065	130.23	mæn ***C***, men ***O*** / were
2066	130.23	bodode / cyðan
	101.6	**nuntiavit**
2067	130.24	*om.* ***C***, ðam ***O*** / him
	101.6	**cui**

2040 Hecht reported *ge[ ]* for *O*. **2050** Hecht gave *reatus* for the Latin (*Einleitung*, p. 161), yet his only acknowledged source, the Maurists' printed edition, has *culpam*. **2067** Hecht reported *þa* for *O*.

2068 130.24 *om. C,* onboden *O* / beboden
101.6 **mandatum**

2069 130.26 hæfde *C,* ongon ... girnan *O* / þohte
101.8 **conatus**

2070 130.28 sceolde / wolde

2071 130.29 drihtnes / godes
101.8 **domini; dei *C***

2072 130.30 witedomes / witegunge
101.8 **prophetiae**

2073 130.32 gehaten *C,* haten *O* / genemned
101.9 **dicebatur**

2074 130.33 gedyde / dyde
101.10 **fecit; iussit Pa_2**

2075 130.34 gyred *C,* gegyred *O* / gescrydd
101.10 **indui**

2076 131.1 hrægle *C,* hræglum *O* / reafum
101.10 **vestibus; vestimentis *Ro***

2077 131.4 on *C, def. O* / to
101.11 **in**

2078 131.4 sende / asende
101.13 **misit**

2079 131.5 ealdormęn *C,* ealdormen *O* / þegenas
101.13 **comites**

2080 131.6 fylgdon *C,* gefulg[ ] *O* / to geþeodde
101.12 **adherere**

2081 131.6 beforan / toforan
101.12 **prae**

2082 131.14 gegearwode / funde
101.16 **praebuit**

2083 131.18 godwebbenum *C,* godwebum *O* / pællenum
101.16 **purpureis**

2084 131.18 hræglum / reafum
101.17 **vestibus**

2085 131.19 gegered *C,* gegyred *O* / gescrydd

2086 131.21 hræglum / reafum
101.18 **vestibus**

2087 131.21 gangende *C,* goncgende *O* / stop
101.19 **-gressus**

2088 131.25 lociende on / behealdende
101.20 **conspiciens**

2089 131.26 gangende *C,* gioncgende *O* / cumendan
101.19 **venientem**

2090 131.26 þa / eallunga
101.20 **iam**

2091 131.28 þam / him
101.20 **eo**

2092 131.31 sona / þærrihte
101.22 **protinus**

2093 131.33 bysmrode / don to bysmore
101.22 **inludere**

2094 132.6 eft / ongean
101.25 **re-**

2095 132.7 bodedon ⁊ sædon (sægdum *O*) / cyddan
101.25 **nuntiaverunt**

2096 132.9 wæron / wurdon
101.26 **fuerant**

2097 132.13 næs ... beald / dorste
102.2 **ausus**

2098 132.13 ganne *C,* gande *O* / genealæcean
102.2 **-cedere**

2099 132.15 *om. C,* ðam *O* / him
102.3 **cui**

2100 132.18 aræred / arisan
102.4 **erigi; ereri St_1**

2101 132.20 wæs / wearð
102.6 **est**

2102 132.23 ahof / arærde
102.6 **levavit**

2103 132.24 cidde *C, def. O* / ofercidde
102.7 **increpavit**

2104 132.27 manega *C,* [ ]onige *O* / fela
102.8 **multa**

2105 132.27 wyrcest *C,* wyrceð *O* / gewyrycst
102.8 **facis**

2106 132.28 manigu *C,* monige *O* / fela
102.9 **multa**

2107 132.28 worhtest *C,* wor[ ] *O* / geworhtest
102.9 **fecisti**

2108 132.28 geara ær *C, def. O* / on sumne sæl
102.9 **aliquando**

2069 Hecht reported *ongan* for *O.* **2080** When undamaged, *O* presumably read *gefulgon;* cf. 161.17 *gefeolað* C, *gefyllað* O: 121.13 *adherent* (quoted by Bosworth-Toller, *Supplement:* see under *gefeolan* II (2)). Hecht reported *geful[ ].* **2100** Waitz reported *erigi* for St_1 (527.22).

2109 132.29 gestyran / gewyld
102.9 **conpescere; desine** *as a gloss La*, **conquiesce** *Maurists, var.*
2110 132.29 unrihtum ***C***, unrihte ***O*** / unrihtwisnysse
102.9 **iniquitate**
2111 132.31 7 ***C***, ***def. O*** / witodlice
102.9 **et quidem; equidem** *Maurists*
2112 132.31 gangende ***C***, [ ]angende ***O*** / becymst
102.10 **-gressurus**
2113 132.31 to / into
102.10 **in-**
2114 133.2 wæs / wearð
2115 133.3 swiðlice ***C***, swyðlice ***O*** / swiðe þearle
102.11 **vehementer**
2116 133.3 abreged / ablyçged
102.11 **territus**
2117 133.3 gewilnode ***C***, gewilnade ***O*** / abedenre
102.12 **petita**
2118 133.5 onweg ***C***, onwæg ***O*** / þanon
102.12 **re-**
2119 133.6 swiðe / eallunga
102.12 **iam**
2120 133.6 unwælgrim / læs wælhreow
102.13 **minus crudelis**
2121 133.7 lytlum ***C***, noht miclum ***O*** / unmycelum
102.13 **non multo**
2122 133.8 gesohte / becom to
102.13 **adiit**
2123 133.9 ealande / iglande
2124 133.15 7 onufon þæt ***C***, ond ufan þæt ***O*** / syððon
102.15 **praeterea**
2125 133.17 com / becuman
103.1 **venire**
2126 133.18 drihtnes / godes
103.1 **domini; dei** *Cl*
2127 133.26 ma / leng
103.5 **amplius**
2128 133.27 þam / him
103.5 **cui**
2129 133.28 byð / wyrð
2130 133.30 for / mid
103.6 **a**
2131 133.30 hreonessum / stormum
103.6 **tempestatibus**
2132 133.31 for / mid
103.6 [a]
2133 134.1 eorðstyrenum ***C***, eorðstyringum ***O*** / eorðstyrungum
103.7 **terrae motu; terrmoto** *St_2*
2134 134.2 weornað (weosnað ***O***) 7 brosnaþ / forweornað
103.8 **marciscit** *M*
2135 134.3 þæs / ðysre
103.8 **cuius**
2136 134.3 witedomes / witegunge
103.8 **prophetiae**
2137 134.4 nu geo (iu ***O***) / eallunga
103.9 **iam**
2138 134.4 swiþe / swutollice
103.9 **luce**
2139 134.5 sceawiað / geseoð
103.11 **cernimus**
2140 134.7 tolysede ***C***, tolysde ***O*** / tohrorene
103.9 **dissoluta; desolata** *V_2*
2141 134.9 getimbru / getimbrunga
103.11 **aedificia**
2142 134.11 gewacode / awacode
103.11 **lassata**
2143 134.11 forð ... gehrorene / tofeallenne
103.12 **prosternantur**
2144 134.12 fyllum ***C***, feallum ***O*** / hryrum
103.11 **ruinis**
2145 134.13 þeah þe / swaþeah
103.12 **quamvis; tamen** *Bo*
2146 134.14 geongra ***C***, geonra ***O*** / leorningcnihtes
103.13 **discipulus**
2147 134.16 spelle / gereccednysse
103.13 **relatione; relatu** *Hf*
2148 134.16 wæs ***C***, w[ ] ***O*** / wearð
103.13 **est**
2149 134.17 7 eac / ac
103.14 **sed**
2150 134.17 þis / hit
103.14 **hoc**

2132 Both versions of the translation repeat *for* or *mid*, rendering the single Latin preposition *a*.

2151 134.18 þæt *C, def. O* / þe
103.14 *om.;* **quod** V_2
2152 134.18 cyðde *C, def. O* / cwæð
103.15 **testatur**
2153 134.19 gebroðrum / broðrum
103.15 **fratribus**
2154 134.22 tid / timan
103.16 **tempore**
2155 134.24 wæs / wearð
2156 134.24 deofle / deofolseocnysse
103.17 **daemonio**
2157 134.24 geswenced / gedreht
103.17 **vexabatur**
2158 134.25 wæs *C, def. O* / wearð
103.18 **fuerat**
2159 134.25 se *C, def. O* / he
103.17 **qui**
2160 134.31 to þon / midþam
2161 134.31 cyðdon *C,* gecyðdon *O* / geswutelodon
104.3 **demonstrarent; agnusceretur** *M*
2162 134.32 godes / halgan
104.3 *om.;* **dei** *Hf*
2163 134.33 wæs / wearð
104.3 **est**
2164 135.9 næfre *C,* nænig *O* / nan
104.6 **non**
2165 135.9 7 / ne
104.7 **vero; et** *Maurists*
2166 135.9 geneð / gedyrstlæc
104.8 **praesumas**
2167 135.10 ga / genealæce
104.7 **accedere**
2168 135.15 sona / þærrihte
104.9 **statim**
2169 135.19 abregeð / gebregeð
104.10 **terrere**
2170 135.20 heold / geheold
104.11 **custodivit**
2171 135.20 bebodu / þing
104.11 **ea**
2172 135.23 ac / soðlice
104.12 **viro** *M*
2173 135.26 *om. C,* ofer *O* / toforan
104.13 **super-**
2174 135.27 swa swa / swylce
104.14 **quasi**
2175 135.30 geeode (gegeode *O*) baldlice / genealæhte
104.15 **accessit**
2176 135.32 eft genam (genom *O*) / gelæhte
104.16 **tenuit**
2177 135.33 ablann *C,* blan *O* / geswac
104.17 **cessavit**
2178 136.2 feorh / sawle
104.16 **animam**
2179 136.2 aþrang *C,* oðþrang *O* / asceoc
104.17 **-cuterit** *M*
2180 136.2 of / fram
104.17 **ex-**
2181 136.4 swylce / ðæs þe
104.18 **etiam**
2182 136.4 þurheode *C,* þurhleornode *O* / þurhferde
104.19 **penetravit**
2183 136.7 gif *C, def. O* / þæt
104.20 **ne**
2184 136.10 7swarode / cwæð
2185 136.11 forhwan *C,* forhwon *O* / hwi
104.21 **quare**
2186 136.11 deogolnysse *C, def. O* / diglan þing
104.21 **secreta**
2187 136.12 *om. C,* godcundan sceawunge *O*/ godcundnysse
104.21 **divinitatis**
2188 136.14 *om. C,* ge[ ]nesse *O* / godcundnysse
104.21 **divinitatis**
2189 136.14 midþy *C,* mitty *O* / þonne
104.22 **cum**
2190 136.15 fylgeð *C,* gefiliegð *O* / geþeodeð to
104.22 **adherit** *M*

2151 *C* abbreviates ꝥ. **2166** *O* has *geneðu*, beside *C*'s *geneð þu.* **2173** Hecht printed *ofergesette* for *O*, beside *H*'s *toforan ... gesette. C* uses another construction with the verb *underfengon.* **2180** Hecht reported *from* for *H.* **2187** *C* has *godcundnysse* only once, corresponding either to *godcundan sceawunge* or to *ge[ ]nesse* in *O.* **2188** When undamaged, *O* probably read *gesetnesse*, as suggested by Hecht. Johnson, however, reported *geo[ ]nesse* for the manuscript (Transcript, p. 107), which, since no more than one or two letters have been lost, allows only *geor(n)nesse* as the restored form.

2191 136.17 nu / gif
104.24 **si**
2192 136.18 folgað *C*, gefolgað *O* / to geþeodeð
104.25 **adherit** *M*
2193 136.22 ungerisenlic *C*, ungerysenlic *O* / unþæslic
105.1 **inconveniens**
2194 137.7 gecyðde / ætywde
105.7 **ostenderet**
2195 137.8 hwylce / þa þing þe
105.8 **quae**
2196 137.9 *om. C*, to *O* / þærto
105.8 **ad-**
2197 137.12 fram *C*, from *O* / of
105.9 **ex**
2198 137.15 þa god *C*, þa ðe *O* / hwylce þing
105.11 **quae**
2199 137.19 ac la / þonne
105.13 **ergo**
2200 137.25 snyttro *C*, snytro *O* / inngehigdes
105.15 **sapientiae**
2201 137.26 unymbfangenlice / unbefangelice
105.16 **inconpraehensibilia**
2202 137.28 sęcgendum *C*, secgendum *O* / sprekendum
105.17 **dicenti**
2203 138.1 hwæt *C*, *def. O* / 7 þonne
105.19 **et cum**
2204 138.1 þæt *C*, *def. O* / hit
2205 138.3 þæt / hit
2206 138.7 nalæs *C*, nallæs *O* / na
105.22 **non**
2207 138.12 hrædnysse *C*, hrædnesse *O* / sceortnysse
105.24 **brevitate**
2208 138.19 beoð / syndon
105.27 **sunt**
2209 138.19 drihtne / gode
105.27 **deo; domino** *Bo*
2210 138.19 þonne / nu
105.27 **adhuc**
2211 138.20 hi / þa
2212 138.20 beoð / syndon
2213 138.20 ahefegode / gehefgode
106.1 **gravati**
2214 138.22 hi / þa
2215 138.22 beoð / syndon
106.1 **sunt**
2216 138.22 drihtne / gode
106.1 **deo; domino** *La*
2217 138.27 cunnon / nyton
106.3 **nesciunt**
2218 138.28 7 *C*, ond *O* / eornostlice
106.3 **enim**
2219 138.28 þonne / nu
106.3 **adhuc**
2220 138.29 þurhleoriað ne ... ongytað *C*, þurhleorniað ne ... ongitað *O* / þurhfarað
106.4 **penetrant**
2221 138.32 unymbfangenlice *C*, unymbefongenlice *O* / unbefangelice
106.4 **inconpraehensibilia**
2222 138.34 ge / oððe
106.6 **vel**
2223 138.35 gesprecum *C*, gespræces *O* / spræcum
106.6 **eloquiis**
2224 139.1 ge eac / oððe
106.6 **vel**
2225 139.3 ongytað *C*, ongitað *O* / oncnawað
106.7 **agnuscunt** *M*
2226 139.4 þas / þa þing
106.7 **haec**
2227 139.5 ac / witodlice
106.8 **igitur; itaque** *Maurists*
2228 139.5 heleð / forsuwað
106.8 **tacit** *M*
2229 139.7 be þan (þon *O*) / 7
106.9 **unde et** (*om. Cl*)
2230 139.10 geecte *C*, geihte *O* / geeacnode
106.10 **-dedit**
2231 139.11 emne swa / swilce
106.10 **ac si**

2200 *CO*'s *snyt(t)ro 7 wisdomes* and *H*'s *wisdomes 7 inngehigdes* render *sapientiae et scientiae* (V_1 omits *et scientiae*). **2220** Hecht reported *þurhleornað* for *O*. **2223** Hecht reported *gespræce* for *O*. **2224** Hecht reported *ge[ ]* for *O*.

2232 139.14 ongæt *C*, ongeat *O* / oncneow
106.12 **cognovi**
2233 139.14 7 / ac
106.12 **nam**
2234 139.15 butan tweon / untwywlice
106.13 **procul dubio**
2235 139.16 ongytenessum *C*, ongitenessum *O* / oncnawennyssum
106.13 **cognitionibus; agnitionibus** *Cl*
2236 139.17 her / herto
2237 139.17 nu / eornostlice
106.13 **ergo**
2238 139.18 wlitelica / witiendlica
106.14 **prophetica**
2239 139.19 7 *C*, [ ]ætte *O* / þæt
106.14 **quia et** (*om.* W_2)
2240 139.20 þonne hwæþre (hwæðere *O*) / swaþeah
106.15 **tamen**
2241 139.25 gelædde / brohte
106.17 **-lata**
2242 139.26 witene *C*, *def. O* / oncnawene
106.16 **scire**
2243 139.29 wearð / is
2244 139.29 cuþ / geopenod
106.18 **patuit**
2245 139.30 wise / intinga
106.18 **causa**
2246 139.32 sęcganne *C*, secganne *O* / wite
2247 139.34 gecyðe / gerecce
106.20 **subiunge**
2248 140.2 7swarode / cwæð
2249 140.3 wæs nama (noma *O*) / genemned
106.22 **nomine**
2250 140.5 geleafan / haligre drohtnunge
2251 140.5 for / þurh
2252 140.5 lare / mynegunge
106.22 **admonitione**
2253 140.6 mid / to
106.23 **apud**
2254 140.7 bælde / truwan
106.23 **fiduciam; gratiam** V_1
2255 140.9 gangende *C*, gongende *O* / eode
106.25 **-gressus**
2256 140.10 in / to ... into
106.25 **in-**
2257 140.14 ablunnon *C*, blunnon *O* / geendodon
106.26 **finiri**
2258 140.15 þonne hwæþre / swaþeah
106.26 **tamen**
2259 140.16 gewunode / gewuna wæs
107.1 **consueverat**
2260 140.19 wise / intinga
107.2 **causa**
2261 140.20 heofes *C*, heafes *O* / wopes
107.2 **luctus**
2262 140.20 þam / him
107.2 **cui**
2263 140.21 hraðe / þærrihte
107.2 **ilico**
2264 140.22 þæt / þe
107.3 **quod**
2265 140.23 wisan / þing
2266 140.26 þeodum / mannum
2267 140.26 beoþ / syndon
108.2 **sunt**
2268 140.26 uneaðe / earfoðlice
108.2 **vix**
2269 140.28 wæron / wurdon
2270 140.28 befæste ... 7 alysde (alyfde *O*) / forgifene
108.3 **cederentur; concederentur** V_2
2271 140.28 þære / þysre
108.2 **hoc**
2272 140.35 gebroðra *C*, gebroðro *O* / broðron
108.6 **fratribus**
2273 141.1 þær / þyder
108.6 **illic**
2274 141.5 nænigne *C*, nænige *O* / nænne
108.7 **ne (nec** *Cl*) **unum**
2275 141.5 gefon / gelæccean
108.8 **tenere**
2276 141.7 gehet / behet
108.9 **promiserat**
2277 141.7 freonde / þeowe
108.8 **famulo**
2278 141.9 feorh / lif
108.9 **animas**

2239 Johnson reported *ðætte* for *O* (Transcript, p. 109). **2241** Hecht printed *forð gelædde* and *forðbrohte.* **2264** *C* and *O* abbreviate ꝥ. **2270** Hecht reported *alysde* for *O.*

2279 141.9 broðra / manna
2280 141.9 gesealde / sealde
108.9 **traderet**
2281 141.11 wisan / þinge
108.10 **re**
2282 141.11 geseo / oncnawe
108.10 **vides**
2283 141.13 geþrowode / þolode
108.11 **pertulit**
2284 141.13 æfwyrdlan *C, def. O* / forwyrd
108.11 **iactura**
2285 141.14 lore *C, def. O* / lyre
108.11 [**iactura**]
2286 141.15 in (*def. O*) him / þæron
2287 141.15 in *C*, i[ ] *O* / to
108.12 **in**
2288 141.21 geleafan / drohtnunge
108.15 **conversum**
2289 141.30 in / be
108.18 **in**
2290 141.30 ahydde / gehydde
108.18 **abscondit**
2291 141.33 oþre / ane
108.19 **unum**
2292 141.34 onfeng / underfeng
108.20 **suscepit**
2293 142.1 manode 7 lærde / warnode
108.20 **monuit; ammonuit** *Ro*
2294 142.2 geseoh *C*, beseah *O* / foresceawa
108.21 **vide**
2295 142.3 in / be
108.21 **de**
2296 142.4 hyddost *C*, ahyddest *O* / gehyddest
108.21 **abscondisti**
2297 142.5 of þære / þærof
2298 142.5 hyld *C*, hyl *O* / ahyld
108.22 **inclina**
2299 142.7 scamiende *C*, scomiende *O* / gescynd 7 ofsceamod
108.22 **confusus**
2300 142.12 þær ... ut / þærut
108.23 **ex-**
2301 142.12 hraðe / hrædlice
108.24 **protinus**
2302 142.13 sumu / an
2303 142.13 gangende *C*, gongende *O* / eode
109.1 **-gressus**
2304 142.14 for / þurh
109.2 **per**
2305 142.17 gedyde / worhte
109.2 **fecit**
2306 142.19 eac / soðlice
109.3 **autem**
2307 142.22 *om. C*, bigonge *O* / bigenge
109.5 **cultu**
2308 142.23 for / þurh
2309 142.27 gewunode *C*, gemende *O* / begymde
109.8 **curabat**
2310 142.28 sænde *C*, sende *O* / asende
109.7 **mittere**
2311 142.33 geþeawe / geþywe
109.8 **more**
2312 142.33 7 *C, def. O* / ac
109.8 **sed**
2313 143.1 þær *C, def. O* / þyder
2314 143.2 gedonan / geendodre
109.9 **factam**
2315 143.3 wæs *C, def. O* / wearð
2316 143.7 swa / þa
109.11 **ut**
2317 143.8 eft cyrrende / ham com
109.11 **reversus**
2318 143.9 mid ... biternesse / biterlice
109.12 **amaritudine**
2319 143.9 swyþlicre *C*, swiðlire *O* / þearle
109.12 **vehementissima**
2320 143.11 unriht / unrihtwisnys
109.13 **iniquitas**
2321 143.12 gangende *C*, gongende *O* / becom
109.13 **ingressa**
2322 143.18 for *C*, from *O* / æt
109.15 **ab; de** V_2
2323 143.19 þa / hi
109.16 **eas**
2324 143.22 hreow / behreowsode
109.17 **poenituit**

2282 De Vogüé has reported *video* for nine of Moricca's manuscripts, all but *M* (p. 334; cited incorrectly as on 108.2). **2285** Both *æfwyrdlan* and *lore*, or *forwyrd* and *lyre*, render *iactura*. **2287** Hecht reported *O* as defective. **2324** De Vogüé has reported *paenituit* for *A* (p. 329).

2325 143.24 ahydde / behydde
109.18 **absconderat**
2326 143.30 sum / an
2327 143.31 rices mannes (mones *O*) / gerefan
109.21 **defensoris**
2328 143.32 candele / leoht
109.22 **lucernam**
2329 143.33 beforan *C*, beforan ... æt ... foran *O* / ætforan
109.21 **ante**
2330 144.2 þæræt / him ætforan
109.23 **ad-**
2331 144.3 candele / leohtes
109.22 **lucernae**
2332 144.4 oferhigdes *C*, oferhygde *O* / oferhogodnysse
109.23 **superbiae**
2333 144.5 þæncan *C*, þencean *O* / wealcan
109.24 **volvere**
2334 144.5 þurh *C*, þur *O* / on
109.24 **per; in *Bo***
2335 144.7 beforan / æt
110.1 **ad-**
2336 144.8 do ... þeowdom / þeowie
110.1 **servitium inpendo**
2337 144.10 þyslicum *C*, þillicum *O* / gelican
110.2 **isti**
2338 144.11 þam / him
110.3 **quem**
2339 144.11 wæs / wearð
2340 144.12 sona / ðærrihte
110.3 **statim**
2341 144.12 gecyrred *C*, gecirred *O* / gehwyrfed
110.3 **conversus**
2342 144.12 swiðlice / swiðe
110.3 **vehementer**
2343 144.15 cwyst oððe þæncest (þencest *O*) / sprycst on ... geþance
110.4 **loqueris**
2344 144.16 þa sona / þærrihte
110.5 **statim**
2345 144.16 cigde *C*, gecigde *O* / clypode
110.5 **vocatis-**
2346 144.17 bebead / het
110.5 **praecepit**
2347 144.18 candele / leoht
110.6 **lucernam**
2348 144.20 gan *C*, agan *O* / gewitan
110.6 **recedere**
2349 144.22 gesæte *C*, *def. O* / sæte
110.7 **sedere**
2350 144.22 wæs / wearð
2351 144.23 gebroðrum *C*, [ ]broðrum *O* / broðrum
110.8 **fratribus**
2352 144.24 gedon ... oððe geþoht / smeade
110.8 **habuerit**
2353 144.26 þurh *C*, þur *O* / be
110.8 **per**
2354 144.28 aþunden *C*, *def. O* / toþunden
110.9 **intumuerat**
2355 144.29 þurh / on
110.10 **per**
2356 144.30 swutollice *C*, [ ]tullice *O* / hluttorlice
110.10 **liquido**
2357 144.31 cuð / geopenod
110.11 **patuit**
2358 144.33 bemiþenes / bediglod
110.11 **latere**
2359 144.34 þæs / his
110.11 **cuius**
2360 144.34 hleoþredon *C*, gehyrdon *O* / swegdon
110.12 **sonuissent**
2361 145.3 eac / witodlice
110.13 **igitur; quoque *S***
2362 145.6 ⁊lyfna *C*, ondlyfena *O* / meteleaste
110.14 **alimentorum**
2363 145.7 þa ... on lande (londe *O*) / landleode
2364 145.9 eac / eallunga
110.16 **viro *M***
2365 145.12 gemette / fundene
110.17 **invenire**
2366 145.13 tid ... gereordnysse (gereordnesse *O*) / gereordungtide
110.17 **refectionis horam**
2367 145.16 geunrotsode / unrote
110.18 **contristatus**
2368 145.16 ongan *C*, ongonn *O* / hogode
110.19 **studuit**
2369 145.17 earfoþnyssa *C*, eaðmodnesse *O* /

		wacmodnysse
	110.19	**posillanimitatem**
2370	145.17	gebetan / þreagenne
	110.19	**corregere**
2371	145.17	gemetfæstlicre / ungemettlicre
	110.19	**modesta**
2372	145.18	þreaunge / ceaste
	110.19	**increpatione**
2373	145.19	gehate / behate
	110.20	**promissione**
2374	145.19	[ongan ***C***, ongonn ***O***] / wolde
	110.19	**[studuit]**
2375	145.19	hyrtan / gehyrtan
	110.20	**sublevare**
2376	145.20	forhwan ***C***, forhwon ***O*** / hwi
	110.20	**quare**
2377	145.20	geunrotsod ***C***, geunrotsad ***O*** / unrot
	110.21	**contristatur**
2378	145.24	þa / soðlice
	110.22	**autem**
2379	145.24	gemetton ***C***, gemeton ***O*** / fundene
	110.23	**inventi**
2380	145.25	beforan ***C***, beforon ***O*** / ætforan
	110.23	**ante**
2381	145.30	geleornodon ***C***, geleornedon ***O*** / ongeaton
	111.3	**dedicerunt**
2382	145.31	sædon ... þancas ***C***, sægdon ... þoncas ***O*** / þanciende
	111.2	**gratias referentes**
2383	145.33	ofer þæt / þa ... eallunga
	111.3	**iam; etiam** V_3
2384	145.33	næron ormode ne ... getweodon (geunrotseden ***O***) / twynienne
	111.4	**dubitare**
2385	145.34	wædle / wædlunge
	111.3	**aegestate**
2386	146.4	witedomes / witegunge
	111.6	**prophetiae**
2387	146.6	witedomes / witegunge
	111.7	**prophetiae**
2388	146.7	7swarode / cwæð
2389	146.8	ealling ***C***, alning ***O*** / simle
	111.10	**semper**
2390	146.8	witedomes / witegunge
	111.9	**prophetiae**
2391	146.10	gecweden / awriten
	111.11	**scriptum; dictum** *Bo*
2392	146.12	eþað / orðað
	111.11	**spirat; aspirat** Pa_2
2393	146.12	forþon / swa
	111.11	**ita**
2394	146.14	geeðað / orðað
	111.12	**adspirat; spirat** O_2
2395	146.27	geændebyrdeð ***C***, geendebyrdeð ***O***/ gedihtnað
	111.19	**disposuit**
2396	146.27	gestihtunge ***C***, gestihtinge ***O*** / gedihtnunge
	111.18	**dispensatione**
2397	146.30	witedomes / witegunge
	111.19	**prophetiae**
2398	146.30	eft wiðtyhð ***C***, ***def.*** ***O*** / oftyhð
	111.20	**subtrahit**
2399	146.31	witegana ***C***, witega ***O*** / witegiendra
	111.20	**prophetantium; prophetarum** *La*
2400	146.32	hwilum / þonne
	111.20	**et**
2401	146.32	ahefð ***C***, ahefeð ***O*** / onfehð
	111.20	**elevat**
2402	146.33	eft / eac
2403	146.36	be / for
	111.22	**de;** ***om.*** V_4
2404	147.1	witedomes / witegunge
	111.22	**prophetiae**
2405	147.4	rihtwisnys ***C***, rihtwisnes ***O*** / gesceadwisnys
	112.1	**ratio**
2406	147.5	cyþeð / cwyð
	112.1	**clamat; declarat** V_3
2407	147.5	þæt / hit

2374 The revision uses *hogode* and *wolde*, corresponding to one expression of *ongan* in the original translation and one expression of *studuit* in the Latin. **2387** Hecht reported that *O* omits a phrase containing *witedomes.* **2395** De Vogüé has reported *disponit* for all the manuscripts used by Moricca, with the possible exception of *M* (p. 334). **2403** Timmer argued that the Latin manuscript used by the reviser lacked *de* (*Studies*, p. 55). None of the other Latin sources collated for the present study omits *de* alone, though St_1 omits the phrase *de Deo.* **2407** *CO*'s ***þæt*** may render the Latin conjunction *ut,* with the subject, corresponding to *H*'s *hit* and

112.1 **hoc**
2408 147.7 sprece / gerecce
112.3 **exequere**
2409 147.13 7swarode / to cwæð
2410 147.17 þegnas / leorningcnihtas
112.6 **discipolis**
2411 147.17 to / on
112.5 **in**
2412 147.19 getrymman ***C***, getimbrian ***O*** / timbrienne
112.6 **construere**
2413 147.24 gewisne fæder / ealdor
112.7 **patrem**
2414 147.26 þam / oðrum
112.8 **eis**
2415 147.27 þyder ***C***, ðider ***O*** / ut
112.8 *om.;* ab- V_2
2416 147.28 gehet / behet
112.8 **spondit; respondit *Maurists, var.***
2417 147.30 gað / farað
112.9 **ite**
2418 147.33 tymbrian ***C***, timbrian ***O*** / aræran
112.11 **aedificare**
2419 147.34 metern ***C***, mete ***O*** / beoddern
112.10 **refectorium**
2420 148.2 hus / inn
112.10 **susceptionem**
2421 148.2 tymbrian ***C***, wyrcean ***O*** / [aræran]
112.11 **[aedificare]**
2422 148.2 swa hwæt swa / gehwilce þing þe
112.11 **quaeque; que** Pa_1
2423 148.3 neodðearflic ***C***, nedþearflic ***O*** / neadbehefe
112.11 **necessaria**
2424 148.3 byþ / syndon
112.11 **sunt; sint *Cl***
2425 148.3 secge ***C***, gesecge ***O*** / gewisie
112.9 **ostendo**
2426 148.5 hraþe / þærrihte
112.12 **ilico**
2427 148.7 neodþearflicu ***C***, neadþearflicu ***O*** / nydbehefe
112.15 **necessaria**
2428 148.10 geornlice / swyðe
112.13 **magnopere**
2429 148.11 anbidiende ***C***, abiddende ***O*** / geanbidiende
112.13 **praestolantes**
2430 148.13 þa / soðlice
112.15 **viro *M***
2431 148.13 gehatena / behatena
112.15 **promissus**
2432 148.15 þeowe / were
112.16 **servo**
2433 148.15 fæder / ealdre
112.16 **patrem**
2434 148.18 smealice ***C***, ***def. O*** / smeaþancollice
112.18 **subtiliter**
2435 148.19 gehwilcum ***C***, gehwylcum ***O*** / syndrigan
112.17 **singula**
2436 148.21 fram ***C***, from ***O*** / of
112.19 **a**
2437 148.21 sædon ***C***, sægdon ***O*** / rehton
112.19 **retulerunt**
2438 148.22 þæt ***C***, ***def. O*** / hwæt
112.19 **quod**
2439 148.23 7 / ac
2440 148.23 na ***C***, no ***O*** / ne
112.20 **non**
2441 148.26 gehet / behet
113.1 **promiserat**
2442 148.30 gnornunge ***C***, grornunge ***O*** / sarinysse
113.2 **merore**
2443 148.32 abidon / geanbidodon
113.3 **expectavimus**
2444 148.33 gehete / behete
113.4 **promiseras**
2445 149.2 *om.* ***C***, hwæt ***O*** / þæt 7 þæt

the Latin's *hoc*, unexpressed. **2414** *H*'s *oðrum* also may help render the Latin participle *secundus.* **2415** Hecht printed *utgangendum* for *H*, beside *CO*'s *gangendum ... þyder.* **2419** *O* has *mete earugian* beside *C*'s *metern wære.* **2421** *CO* repeats *tymbrian* (or *wyrcean*), but the revision expresses *aræran*, and the Latin expresses *aedificare*, only once. **2422** See the note to entry **1063.** **2426** Hecht gave *statim* for the Latin (*Einleitung*, p. 165), yet his only acknowledged source, the Maurists' printed edition, has *illico.* Cf. entries **278** and **1668.**

113.4 **quid**
2446 149.4 þam / him
113.5 **quibus**
2447 149.5 cweðað / secge
113.6 **dicitis**
2448 149.5 ac / hu
113.6 **numquid**
2449 149.6 gehet / behet
113.6 **promisi**
2450 149.9 forhwan *C*, to ðon *O* / hwænne
113.7 **quando**
2451 149.13 gað ... forð (forðon *O*) / farað
113.8 **ite**
2452 149.16 sona / þa
2453 149.18 swiðlice / þearle
113.10 **vehementer**
2454 149.18 gecyrde / gehwurfon
113.11 **-versi**
2455 149.19 cwedenan / sædan
113.11 **-dictum**
2456 149.19 getrymedon / getimbrodon
113.12 **construxerunt**
2457 149.20 in ... mynster (mynstres *O*) / eardungstowa
113.11 **habitacula**
2458 149.26 eode / ferde
113.14 **iret**
2459 149.32 tweost *C*, tweoð *O* / twynast
113.17 **ambigis**
2460 149.33 wisan / þinges
113.16 **rei**
2461 149.34 witudlice *C*, witodlice *O* / gewisslice
113.17 **profecto**
2462 150.2 witon 7 habbaþ / cunnon
113.18 **novimus**
2463 150.2 to / on
2464 150.3 gewitan / gewitnesse
113.18 **teste; testante** V_1
2465 150.4 wæs *C*, *def. O* / wearð
113.19 **est; esset** Pa_2
2466 150.6 underngeweorce *C*, *def. O* / underngereorde
113.19 **prandio**
2467 150.8 metes gereorde *C*, me[ ] *O* / gemete
113.20 **prandio**
2468 150.9 leoneseaðe *C*, leonseaðe *O* / leona seaðe
2469 150.10 semninga *C*, samninga *O* / færinga
113.21 **repente**
2470 150.10 com / gemeted
113.21 **invenit**
2471 150.12 nu / gif
113.21 **si**
2472 150.12 þa / þonne
113.21 **igitur**
2473 150.14 faran / gefaran
113.22 **ire**
2474 150.14 undernmete / underngereord
113.22 **prandium**
2475 150.19 sæde *C*, gesægde *O* / gecyðde
113.25 **narrarit** *M*
2476 150.26 tweon / twynunge
114.1 **dubietatem**
2477 150.27 hulic / hwilc
114.3 **qualis**
2478 151.1 mycelnysse *C*, mycelnesse *O* / byrðene
114.5 **pondere**
2479 151.4 feollon / befeollon
114.6 **cadebant**
2480 151.5 nanra (nane *O*) þinga / natoþæshwon
114.6 **nequaquam**
2481 151.6 ac / soðlice
114.7 **viro** *M*
2482 151.7 bodiende *C*, beotiende *O* / þywende
114.7 **minando**
2483 151.8 þeah þe / eallunga
114.7 **iam**
2484 151.8 eorneste *C*, on eornost *O* / gestihtiende
114.7 **decernendo; diffiniendo** *as a*

2450 Instead of *for hwanne come þu*, as printed by Hecht for *C*, read *forhwan ne cume þu*. For *O*, Hecht reported *to ðon come þu*, but the manuscript actually has *to ðon ne come þu*. **2455** Hecht printed *forecwedenan* and *foresædan*. **2466** Hecht reported *underngeworce* for *C*. **2467** Hecht reported *m[ ]* for *O*. **2469** Hecht reported *sæmninga* for *O*.

gloss Ro

2485 151.8 gecwæde / cwæð
114.7 **diceret**

2486 151.10 word / spræc
114.8 **sermo**

2487 151.11 þæt / hit
114.8 **hoc**

2488 151.11 untweogendlice *C*, untweogenlice *O* / na twyniende
114.8 **non dubiae**

2489 151.11 7 / oððe
114.8 **atque; ac** *Cl*

2490 151.12 buton yldinge *C*, butan yldincge *O* / [na] yldende
114.8 [**non**] **suspense** (**curiose** *as a gloss Ro*)

2491 151.12 7 / ac
114.9 **sed**

2492 151.12 eac eall (ealle *O*) / eallunga
114.9 **iam; etiam** *Cl*

2493 151.12 for / þurh
114.9 **per**

2494 151.14 soðlice / witodlice
114.9 **nam**

2495 151.14 naht feor / unfeorr
114.9 **longe; non longe** *C*

2496 151.18 gegearwode þegnunge (ðegnuncge *O*) 7 hyrsumnesse (hyrsumnysse *O*) / þenode
114.12 **praebebat obsequium**

2497 151.27 syn / beon
114.15 **fuisse**

2498 151.27 ma gode / be dæle beteran
114.14 **plus ... aliquid**

2499 151.27 þonne *C*, *def. O* / toforan

2500 151.28 na *C*, no *O* / ne
114.15 **nec-**

2501 151.29 cwedenan / sædan
114.15 **-dictae**

2502 151.30 geheoldon / heoldon
114.17 **restrinxerant**

2503 151.32 fulloft / foroft
114.18 **saepe**

2504 151.34 se / þe
114.17 **qui**

2505 152.2 nydþearfnessum *C*, nioddðearfnesse *O* / neadþearfum
114.18 **necessaria**

2506 152.3 aræfnode *C*, aræfnde *O* / forbær
114.19 **toleraret**

2507 152.5 sæde *C*, andswarode *O* / asæde
114.21 **enarravit; narravit** V_2

2508 152.5 manigne *C*, monige *O* / fela
114.20 **quantas-**

2509 152.6 orwyrdu ... fracoðwyrda *C*, orwyrðu ... fracoðworda *O* / yfelra worda
114.20 **verborum contumilias**

2510 152.7 geþrowode / geþolode
114.20 **pateretur**

2511 152.9 onbead / bebead
114.22 **mandavit**

2512 152.14 gespræc / gecwæð
114.24 **intulit; loquutus** *as a gloss La*

2513 152.14 þy / forþam
114.23 **quam**

2514 152.15 forðbryngan *C*, forðbrincgan *O* / gelæstan
114.24 **proferendo; praeferendo** *S*

2515 152.16 beotigende *C*, beotiende *O* / þywende
115.1 **intentando; imminando** O_2, **comminando** V_3, **minando** *and* **intendendo** *as glosses La*, **interpretando** *Maurists, var.*

2516 152.16 witudlice *C*, witodlice *O* / soðlice
115.1 **autem**

2517 152.17 nahte (noht *O*) þy ær / nan þing
115.1 **nihil**

2518 152.17 næron / wurdon
115.1 *om.;* **sunt** Pa_2

2519 152.18 fram *C*, from *O* / of
115.1 **a**

2520 152.19 þa / ac

2521 152.21 þa / ðonne
115.2 **cumque**

2522 152.23 weorðode *C*, we[ ]ðode *O* / gewurðode

2490 Wærferth's original translation has *untweogendlice 7 buton yldinge* beside *na twyniende oððe yldende* in the revision and *non dubiae atque suspense* in the Latin. **2501** Hecht printed *forecwedenan* and *foresædan.* **2505** Hecht reported *[ ]dðearfnesse* for *O*.

	115.3	**celebrarentur**
2523	152.24	þa *C*, ðonne *O* / swa
2524	154.8	7swarode / cwæð
2525	154.8	eac / witodlice
	116.11	**quoque**
2526	154.10	cniht ... munuc / munuccnapana
	116.12	**puerolus (*M*) monachus**
2527	154.12	higode / yrnende
	116.13	**tendens**
2528	154.13	ferde / for
	116.13	[**tendens**]
2529	154.18	wæs / wearð
	116.15	**est**
2530	154.18	*om. C*, wæs *O* / wearð
	116.15	**essit** *M*
2531	154.18	eac *C*, midty ... eac *O* / þa
	116.15	**cum-**
2532	154.19	þa / ac
2533	154.21	þane *C*, þonne *O* / þa
2534	154.21	tolæddon *C*, toledon *O* / begymdon
	116.16	**curaverunt**
2535	154.22	byrgene (byrgenne *O*) ... befæstan / bebyrgdon
	116.16	**tradere sepulturae**
2536	154.24	gemetton *C*, gemeton *O* / fundon
	116.18	**invenerunt**
2537	154.26	hraðe *C*, hwæðre *O* / hrædlice
	116.18	**conciti**
2538	154.29	geeadmodod *C*, geeadmodad *O* / gemedemode
	116.20	**dignaretur**
2539	154.30	forgifnysse *C*, forgyfennesse *O* / mildse
	116.20	**gratiam; indulgentiam** *as a gloss Ro*
2540	154.30	sealde / forgeafe
	116.20	**largire**
2541	155.1	cnihte / munuccnapan
2542	155.1	þam *C*, [ ]am *O* / him
	116.20	**quibus**
2543	155.5	gað / farað
	116.21	**ite**
2544	155.6	ofer / uppon
	116.22	**super**
2545	155.8	agyfað ... byrgene *C*, forgyfað ... byrgenne *O* / bebyriað
	116.22	**sepulturae ... tradite**
2546	155.9	geworden / gedon
	116.23	**factus**
2547	155.10	gehæfde / geheold
	116.24	**tenuit**
2548	155.11	onfangenan *C*, onfoncgnan *O* / underfangenan
	116.23	**susceptum**
2549	155.16	nu / þæt
	116.25	**ut**
2550	155.18	forgyfnesse *C*, forgyfennesse *O* / mildsunge
	117.1	**gratiam**
2551	155.19	swyþlice *C*, swiðlice *O* / swiðe
	117.3	**vehementer**
2552	155.23	7swarode *C*, andswarode *O* / cwæð
2553	155.27	midþy / þa
	117.6	**cumque**
2554	155.28	cidde *C*, ofercidde *O* / mynegode
	117.6	**corriperet (corrigeret *C*/) ... admoneret**
2555	155.30	nanum (nane *O*) gemete ... to þon / natoþæshwon
	117.7	**nullo modo**
2556	155.31	hyran *C*, hyra *O* / geþwærode
	117.7	**consentiret**
2557	156.1	fylgede *C*, fylgde *O* / befealh
	117.9	**inminerit** *M;* **insisteret** *as a gloss Ta*
2558	156.2	bedum *C*, *def. O* / benum
	117.8	**precibus**
2559	156.5	wæs *C*, *def. O* / wearð
2560	156.6	unluste / gedrefednysse
	117.10	**taedio**
2561	156.6	geornnesse *C*, geornesse *O* / onhropes
	117.9	**nimietatis**
2562	156.10	sumne / anne
2563	156.12	*om. C*, se *O* / þe
	117.12	**qui**
2564	156.14	forhtiende / ofdrædd bifian

2528 Both *higode* and *ferde*, or *yrnende* and *for*, render *tendens*. 2531 Hecht reported *mit ty* for *O*. 2532 Hecht reported that *O* omits *þa*. 2546 De Vogüé has reported *factum* for *A* (p. 331). 2554 *CO*'s *(ofer)cidde* probably renders *corriperet; H*'s *mynegode, admoneret.*

	117.13	**tremens**
2565	156.14	bredetende *C*, brocciende *O* / broddettan
	117.13	**palpitans**
2566	156.15	stefnum / hreame
	117.13	**vocibus**
2567	156.19	nænigne / nænne
	117.15	**menime**
2568	156.20	byfiende *C*, bifiende *O* / cwakiendne
	117.16	**trementem**
2569	156.23	sona *C*, *om. O* / þærrihte
	117.17	**statim**
2570	156.23	gehet *C*, *om. O* / behet
	117.17	**promisit**
2571	156.24	þa / eac
	117.18	**ad-**
2572	156.26	gehatum / behate
	117.18	**promissione**
2573	156.26	7 (ond *O*) þa swa / witodlice
	117.19	**quippe**
2574	157.2	eac / ac
	117.21	**sed**
2575	157.2	þis / þæt
	117.21	**hoc**
2576	157.3	ongæt *C*, ongeat *O* / oncneow
	117.22	**cognovi; agnovi** V_4
2577	157.4	æþelan / mæran
	117.21	**inlustri**
2578	157.4	he *C*, ðe *O* / se
2579	157.4	hit / þis
2580	157.5	sæde *C*, sægde *O* / rehte
	117.22	**narrante**
2581	157.5	se / he
	117.22	**qui**
2582	157.6	hreofan / hreofligan
	117.23	**elefantino**
2583	157.8	asweoll / tosweoll
	118.1	**intumisceret**
2584	157.9	swa / to þam
	118.1	**atque**
2585	157.10	wyrms 7 wiðl *C*, wurms 7 widl *O* / wyrmsi
	118.1	**saniem**
2586	157.11	wæs / wearð
	118.3	**est**
2587	157.18	swigian *C*, swige *O* / forsuwie
	118.5	**taceam**
2588	157.19	sæde *C*, sægde *O* / reccenne
	118.6	**narrare**
2589	157.22	geneded *C*, genieded *O* / geþrafod
	118.7	**conpulsus**
2590	157.22	getreowe / geleaffull
	118.6	**fidelis**
2591	157.25	læcedom / helpe
	118.7	**remedium**
2592	157.26	were / þeowe
	118.8	**virum**
2593	157.27	neod *C*, nyd *O* / neadung
	118.9	**necessitas**
2594	157.28	þreade / þreatode
	118.8	**urguerit** *M*
2595	157.28	com / becom
	118.9	**venit**
2596	157.33	fore *C*, *def. O* / for
	118.11	**pro**
2597	157.33	þam / him
	118.11	**cui**
2598	158.1	sæde *C*, [ ]de *O* / cwæð
	118.12	**respondit**
2599	158.2	nanra þinga *C*, nane þincga *O* / natoþæshwon
	118.12	**nequaquam**
2600	158.3	þonne (*def. O*) hwæþre / swaþeah
	118.13	**tamen**
2601	158.5	afrefrode *C*, afr[ ] *O* / gefrefrode
	118.13	**consolatus**
2602	158.5	ymb *C*, ymbe *O* / æfter
	118.14	**post**
2603	158.6	niht *C*, neiht *O* / dagum
	118.14	**biduum**
2604	158.8	soðlice / 7
	118.15	**autem**
2605	158.9	nihtum / dagum
	118.15	**biduo**
2606	158.9	wæs / wearð
	118.15	**fuit; est** *Ro*
2607	158.13	semninga / færinga

2567 De Vogüé has reported *minime* for *A* (p. 329, n. 13). **2582** Hecht reported *hreoflican* for *H*.
2590 Hecht reported *getreow* for *O*.

118.18 **subito**
2608 158.17 þa / hi
118.18 **quos**
2609 158.18 cwæð / het
118.19 **dicens**
2610 158.21 nytte / behofe
118.20 **expensis *C;* inpensis *changed to* expensis *Cl***
2611 158.22 cyrre *C*, cerre *O* / gecyrre
118.21 **-eam**
2612 158.22 ongeat / oncneow
118.22 **agnovi**
2613 158.23 fruman / foreweardre
118.22 **exordio**
2614 158.24 sædon *C*, sægdon *O* / rehton
118.22 **referentibus**
2615 158.25 wunne / swunce
118.23 **laborabat**
2616 158.33 tobræded *C*, tobrocen *O* / togoten
119.1 **diffusa *C***
2617 159.2 hreof / hreofli
119.1 **leprae**
2618 159.3 *om. C*, wæs *O* / wearð
2619 162.1 scylde / gylt
121.23 **culpam; poenam O_2**
2620 162.2 forþon / openlice
121.24 **ergo**
2621 162.3 þas / þa
121.24 **haec**
2622 162.4 doð / gegearwiað
121.24 **exhibent**
2623 162.5 midþy *C*, mytty *O* / forðam
121.25 **dum**
2624 162.6 þysum *C*, ðissum *O* / þam
121.25 **istis**
2625 162.6 cwedenum *C*, cwedenan *O* / leogendum
2626 162.7 afyrde *C*, afirde *O* / afyrsode
121.25 **abstulit**
2627 162.8 mid ... gebedum (gebed[ ] *O*) / gebiddende
122.1 **orando**
2628 162.9 witodlice / soðlice
122.1 **nam**
2629 162.13 scineþ *C*, scin[ ] *O* / swutelað
122.2 **clareat**
2630 162.15 fram (from *O*) gode / godcundlice
122.3 **divinitus**
2631 162.18 wæs nama / genemned
122.5 **nomine**
2632 162.22 abarn ⁊ aweoll / ontend
122.8 **exarsit**
2633 162.23 unmætestan *C*, unmættesta[ ] *O*/ ormætestan
122.7 **inmanissimae**
2634 162.25 ęallæcan *C*, halegan *O* / geleaffullre
122.6 **catholicae**
2635 162.26 cyrican *C*, ciricean *O* / gelaðunge
122.7 **aecclesiae**
2636 162.27 com ([ ]com *O*) to / becom
122.8 **venissit *M;* advenisset *Bo***
2637 162.27 [to] ... beforan / toforan
122.8 **ante; ante ... [ad-] *Bo***
2638 162.28 nanra þinga *C*, nane ðincga *O* / nateshwon
122.9 **nullo modo**
2639 162.29 cwic / libbende
122.9 **vivus**
2640 162.30 onbærned / onæled
122.10 **succensus**
2641 162.32 higiende *C*, hogiende *O* / grædig
122.11 **inhians**
2642 162.32 gestrude *C*, gestreone *O* / reaflace
122.10 **rapinam**
2643 163.4 wundode / cwylmde
122.12 **laniaret**
2644 163.4 missenlicu / menifealde
122.12 **diversa**
2645 163.7 æhte / þing
122.13 **res**
2646 163.9 dyde / sæde
2647 163.9 he / se
2648 163.10 tintregiendan *C*, tintregien[ ]m *O*/

2633 Johnson reported *unmættestan* for *O* (Transcript, p. 127). 2634 Hecht reported *æallæcan* for *C*. 2637 *CO* has *com to him beforan his onsyne* beside *H's becom toforan his ansyne* and the Latin's *ante faciem (ad)venissit.* 2648 When undamaged *O* presumably read *tintregiendum.* In fact, a minim remains visible

cwylmend
122.14 **torquente**
2649 163.13 beon / wurde
2650 163.13 gehyrted / genered
122.15 **raperentur**
2651 163.15 ablan *C*, blon *O* / geswac
122.16 **cessavit**
2652 163.20 cyþde / geswutelode
122.18 **demonstraret**
2653 163.22 eode / stop
122.19 **-cedens**
2654 163.23 þam *C*, þone *O* / him
122.19 **quem**
2655 163.26 beforan / ætforan
122.20 **ante**
2656 163.27 dura ... cytan / mynstergeate
122.20 **ingressum cellae**
2657 163.34 þæs / his
2658 163.36 brogan / ege
122.24 **terrore**
2659 164.1 stefnum / hreame
123.1 **vocibus; clamoribus** *Pa*$_1$
2660 164.4 æhta *C*, æhte *O* / yddisce
123.2 **res**
2661 164.5 drihtnes / godes
123.3 **dei; domini** *Ro*
2662 164.6 hraðe *C*, raðe *O* / hrædlice
123.3 **protinus**
2663 164.7 þone / hine
123.3 **eum-**
2664 164.8 swa / midþam þe
2665 164.10 þæs / his
123.5 **cuius**
2666 164.14 nanra þinga *C*, na[ ]þincga *O* / ne
123.7 **nulla**
2667 164.15 ænigre / nanes
123.7 [**nulla**]
2668 164.15 efestinge *C*, æfæstþincge *O* / ofste
123.7 **festinatione**
2669 164.16 undon 7 unwriðene *C*, ondo[ ] 7 onwriðenne *O* / tolysede
123.7 **dissolvi**
2670 169.7 gangende *C*, gande *O* / agane
127.24 **-gressam**
2671 169.8 ansyne *C*, onsyne *O* / hiwe
127.24 **speciae**
2672 169.10 7 *C*, ond *O* / hwæt
2673 169.10 efengefeande *C*, efengefeonde *O* / efenblissiende
128.1 **congaudens**
2674 169.11 wundres / wuldres
128.1 **gloriae**
2675 169.12 dyde þancas (þoncas *O*) / þancode
128.2 **gratias reddedit**
2676 169.13 ymnum / ymensangum
128.2 **hymnis**
2677 169.13 sæde (sægde *O*) ... 7 bodode / cyðde
128.3 **denuntiavit; enuntiavit** *O*$_1$
2678 169.14 forðfore / forðsið
128.2 **obitum**
2679 169.15 sænde *C*, sende *O* / asennde
128.3 **misit**
2680 169.15 sona / hrædlice
128.3 **protinus**
2681 169.15 þa / hi
128.3 **quos**
2682 169.19 geteohhode (getihhode *O*) 7 geworhte / gegearwode
128.5 **paraverat**
2683 169.19 þa *C*, ðy *O* / ðysum
128.5 **quo** *C*
2684 169.22 heora *C*, hiora *O* / þara
128.6 **eorum**
2685 169.26 sume / oðrum
128.8 **alio**
2686 169.26 tide / timan
128.8 **tempore**
2687 169.28 þæt / þe
128.9 **quod**
2688 170.1 com / becom
128.11 **convenerat**

before the *m*. **2656** Hecht reported *[ ]ura* for *O*. **2666** *O* undamaged probably read *nane þincga;* see entry **176** and note. **2667** Both *nanra þin(c)ga* and *ænigre*, or *ne* and *nanes*, may render *nulla*. **2668** Hecht reported *efæstþincge* for *O*. **2670** Hecht printed *utgangende*, *utgande*, and *ut agane*. **2674** Hecht reported *wundre* for *O*. **2676** *O* reads *gode[ ]n ymnum*, rather than *gode[ ]hymnum*, as reported by Hecht. **2687** *C* and *O* abbreviate ꝥ.

2689 170.1 mid / for

2690 170.2 gife *C*, gyfe *O* / þingon
128.10 **gratia**

2691 170.3 7 / witodlice
128.11 **quippe**

2692 170.3 geneahhe / gelomlice
128.11 **frequentabat**

2693 170.5 sænden *C*, sendon *O* / on aguton
128.13 **transfunderent**

2694 170.5 betweoh *C*, betwih *O* / betwynon gemænelice
128.13 **invicem**

2695 170.5 wynsuman *C*, wunsuman *O* / swetan
128.13 **dulcia**

2696 170.7 swetan / wynsuman
128.13 **suavem**

2697 170.9 geseonde / geblissiende
128.14 **gaudendo**

2698 170.10 huru ... hwæthugu (tohwega *O*) / huruþinga
128.15 **saltim**

2699 170.13 mid / on
128.12 **in-; af-** *V_1*

2700 170.14 midþy *C*, mitty *O* / soðlice ... eallunga
128.15 **viro (*M;* -que *Maurists*) ... iam**

2701 170.14 wæs / becom
128.16 **exegerit** *M*

2702 170.14 tid / tima
128.15 **hora**

2703 170.16 gestaþolode *C*, gestaðelod[ ] *O* / gelogode
128.18 **conlocavit**

2704 170.17 uferan dælum / upflora
128.16 **superioribus**

2705 170.18 þæs / sumes
128.16 **cuius; eius** *Bo*

2706 170.18 torres / stypeles
128.16 **turris**

2707 170.19 gestaþelode / gereste
128.18 [**conlocavit**]

2708 170.20 neoðeran (nyðoran *O*) dælum / nyðerflore
128.17 **inferioribus**

2709 170.21 torres / stypeles
128.16 [**turris**]

2710 170.21 witodlice / 7
128.18 **videlicit** *M*

2711 170.22 nyþeran dæle *C*, nioþeran dælum *O* / nyðerflora
128.18 **inferiore**

2712 170.23 uferan [dæle (dælum *O*)] / upflora
128.18 **superioribus**

2713 170.23 samodgang *C*, somedtoncg *O* / trum stæger
128.19 **continuabat; coniunxit** *as a gloss Ro*

2714 170.23 þurh / mid
128.19 *om.;* **per** *M*

2715 170.24 upstige *C*, [ ]pstige *O* / stapum
128.19 **ascensus**

2716 170.24 soðlice / eac
128.19 **viro** *M*

2717 170.24 beforan / ætforan
128.19 **ante**

2718 170.25 torre / stypele
128.19 **turrem**

2719 170.25 swiþe / sum

2720 170.26 ægþres / begra
128.20 **utriusque**

2721 170.26 þenas *C*, ðegnas *O* / gingran
128.20 **discipuli**

2722 170.27 midþy *C*, *def. O* / ða þa
129.1 **cumque**

2723 170.29 tide / timan
129.2 **tempora**

2690 Hecht reported *[ ]e* for *O*. **2695** Hecht reported *wun[ ]rlican* for *O*, as did Johnson (Transcript, p. 135). **2697** Hecht reported *gefeonde* for *O*. **2707** To render *conlocavit*, the original translation repeats *gestaþelode*, the revision uses *gelogode* and *gereste*. **2709** Both versions of the translation repeat *torres* or *stypeles*, though the Latin expresses *turris* only once. **2711** De Vogüé has reported *inferiora* for all the manuscripts used by Moricca, with the possible exception of *M* (p. 334). **2712** The original translation has *fram þam nyþeran dæle in* (om. *O*) *to þam uferan* beside the revision's *fram þære nyðerflora to þære upflora*. **2713** The Latin's *pervius (per huius* M*) continuabat ascensus* corresponds to *wæs samodgang þurh gewisne upstige* / *wæs ... trum stæger mid gewissum stapum;* see Harting, p. 295 and n. 1. **2715** Hecht reported *[ ]stige* for *O*.

2724 170.29 þæs / his

2725 170.30 gefealh ... wæcce (wacone *O*) / þurhwacol
129.2 **instans vigiliis**

2726 170.31 standende / gestod
129.3 **stans**

2727 170.32 þam / anum

2728 170.32 gebiddende ... to / biddende
129.3 **depraecans**

2729 170.34 semninga *C*, semnincga *O* / færinga
129.4 **subito**

2730 170.34 tid / timan
129.4 **hora**

2731 170.34 stillan / stillnysse
129.4 **intempesta**

2732 171.1 forð / ut
129.4 **re-**

2733 171.2 aflyman *C*, geflyman *O* / afligean
129.5 **exfugasse**

2734 171.3 nihte *C*, neahte *O* / nihtlican
129.5 **noctis**

2735 171.6 þæt / þe
129.6 **quae**

2736 171.7 eala þæt / hwæt þa
129.7 **autem**

2737 171.8 wise / þing
129.7 **res**

2738 171.10 æfter þam (ðon *O*) / syððan
129.8 **post**

2739 171.11 sæde *C*, sægde *O* / rehte
129.8 **narravit**

2740 171.12 swa swa / swylce
129.9 **velut**

2741 171.12 leoman (leoma[ ] *O*) ... sunnan / sunnanleoman
129.9 **solis radio**

2742 171.13 gegaderod *C*, gegeagrad *O* / gelogod
129.9 **collectus**

2743 171.16 geornfullan *C*, geor[ ] *O* / atihtan
129.10 **intentam**

2744 171.16 gesihþe *C*, gesyhðe *O* / scearpnysse
129.11 **aciem**

2745 171.17 leoman / beorhtnesse
129.11 **splendore**

2746 171.22 berende *C*, bo[ ]ne *O* / ferian
129.13 **ferri; deferri** O_1

2747 171.22 in / into
129.13 **in**

2748 171.23 begytan / gelangian
129.13 **adhibere**

2749 171.25 cigde / clypode
130.2 **vocavit**

2750 171.26 *om.* *C*, eft *O* / oft hrædlice
130.1 **iterato**

2751 171.28 cleopunge *C*, cleopuncge *O* / hreames
130.2 **clamoris**

2752 171.30 myccles (micles *O*) 7 ... arwyrþes / mæres
130.3 **tanti**

2753 171.31 þa / 7

2754 171.31 stah *C*, stag *O* / astah
130.3 **-scendit**

2755 171.32 forþ / þyder
130.3 **re-**

2756 171.32 þa / eallunga
130.4 **iam**

2757 171.33 mycelne *C*, medmicelne *O* / lytelne
130.4 **exiguam**

2758 172.2 sæde *C*, asægde *O* / gerehte
130.5 **narravit**

2759 172.2 æfter / be
130.5 **per**

2760 172.3 wisan / þing

2761 172.4 gedone / gewordene
130.5 **gesta**

2762 172.4 þa sona / þærrihte
130.5 **statim-**

2763 172.5 stowe *C*, stoc *O* / stocwic
130.6 **castrum**

2764 172.5 onbead / bebead
130.6 **mandavit**

2765 172.9 ongeate *C*, ongyte *O* / gewiste

2730 Hecht reported *O* as defective. 2735 *C* and *O* abbreviate ꝥ. 2746 When undamaged, *O* presumably read either *borne*, as suggested by Hecht, or *borene;* cf. *borene* CO (272.15) and *geborene* CO (151.16, 261.20, 261.23). 2765 De Vogüé has reported *agnosceret* for *A* (p. 330).

130.8 **agnusceret**
2766 172.10 gebude / gecyðde
130.8 **indicaret**
2767 172.12 gedon *C, def. O* / geworden
130.9 **factum-**
2768 172.15 þa / eallunga
130.10 **iam**
2769 172.16 ongeat / oncneow
130.11 **agnovit**
2770 172.17 tid / timan
130.11 **momento**
2771 172.18 forðfore *C*, forðfor *O* / forðsið
130.11 **obitum**
2772 172.21 wise / þing
130.13 **res**
2773 172.21 þæt / þis
2774 172.21 eac / ac
130.13 **sed**
2775 172.21 swiþe / þearle
130.13 **vehementer**
2776 172.23 swa swa / swylce
130.14 **quasi**
2777 172.24 leoman / sunnanleoman
130.14 **solis radio**
2778 172.27 ongytende *C*, ongitende *O* / gemunde
130.16 **expertus; inveni** *as a gloss La*
2779 172.27 7swarian *C*, swa geradelice *O* / beþencean
130.16 **conicere; aestimare** *as a gloss La*
2780 172.29 þæt / hit
2781 172.32 7swarode / to cwæð
2782 172.32 nim / genim
130.18 **tene**
2783 173.6 byþ *C*, bið *O* / is
130.21 **est**
2784 173.8 sceat / bosum
130.22 **sinus**
2785 173.9 toleoðod *C*, toliðod *O* / tolæten
130.21 **laxatur; elaxatur** W_2
2786 173.9 swa / to þam
130.22 **tantum-**
2787 173.10 tobræded / gebræded
130.22 **expanditur**
2788 173.11 ufor / hyhra ofer
130.22 **superior**
2789 173.14 genumen / gegripen
130.24 **rapitur**
2790 173.16 gebræded / tobræded
130.24 **ampliatur**
2791 173.18 ongyteð *C*, ongitað *O* / oncnæwð
130.25 **conpraehendit; intellegit** *as a gloss La*
2792 173.19 þe / þæt
130.26 **quod**
2793 173.20 ymbfon 7 oncnawan / ongitan
130.26 **conpraehendere**
2794 173.22 gehæfd 7 gehyned *C*, hæfd 7 heledu *O* / geeaðmodad
130.26 **humiliata**
2795 173.22 soðlice / eornostlice
130.26 **ergo**
2796 173.24 swylce *C*, swilce *O* / eac
131.1 **quoque**
2797 173.26 buton (butan *O*) tweon / untwylice
131.2 **procul dubio**
2798 173.32 middangeard / middaneard
131.4 **mundum**
2799 173.34 þær *C, def. O* / þæt
2800 174.1 middangeard / middaneard
131.5 **mundus**
2801 174.4 tosomne / togædere
131.6 **con-**
2802 174.6 to / on
131.6 **in**
2803 174.9 þe *C, om. O* / þæt
131.7 **quod**
2804 174.10 forþon / eornostlice
131.8 **ergo** *C*
2805 174.11 sceawunge / leohte
131.8 **luce**
2806 174.11 seo / þe
131.8 **quae**
2807 174.11 acsung *C*, acsuncg *O* / scean
131.8 **fulsit**
2808 174.14 genam *C*, genom *O* / gegrap
131.10 **rapuit**
2809 174.15 uferan / upplicum
131.9 **superiora**

2789 Hecht reported *ge[ ]en* for *O*. 2792 *H* abbreviates *ꝥ*. 2794 Hecht reported *[ ]eledu(?)* for *O*. 2799 *H* abbreviates *ꝥ*. 2803 *H* abbreviates *ꝥ*.

2810 174.15 wisan / þingum
2811 174.16 gecyþde / geswutelode
131.10 **monstravit**
2812 174.17 ænge *C*, encge *O* / gehwæde
131.10 **angusta**
2813 174.19 ongyte / undergite
131.11 **intellexisse**
2814 174.20 fornytlice 7 nydþearflice (nedðearflice *O*) / full nyttlice
131.11 **utiliter**
2815 174.21 word / þing
2816 174.21 þa þe *C*, þa þa *O* / þonne
131.12 **quando**
2817 174.23 fram *C*, from *O* / of
131.12 **ex**

2811 Hecht printed *gewutelode* in the text, then corrected it to *geswutelode* in his 'Berichtigungen' (after p. 374).

word index

For alphabetizing, þ = th; ę immediately follows æ, which = ae; 7 immediately follows and. þ/ð variation is not recorded: each word takes its form from the first entry cited from the thesaurus. See pages xxi and xxii of the Introduction for an explanation of the asterisk (*) or dagger (†) that accompanies some numbers. The different forms of individual words are cross-referenced, as are any closely related words not cross-referenced in Bosworth-Toller-Campbell.